I Hope you'll enjoy reading this story
Allen Hern (Papa?)

A GOOD HERITAGE

The Story of Lew and Mabel Hern

ALLEN HERN

A Good Heritage
Copyright © 2020 by Allen Hern

Tellwell Talent
www.tellwell.ca

ISBN
978-0-2288-3672-8 (Paperback)

Preface to "A Good Heritage"

s a pastor, I have often encouraged older people to write down their story so that their loved ones might have an understanding of their family background. What is not recorded before we leave this life is lost forever.

My mother in her later years wrote down her memories several times, over and over, on three ringed notepaper, so I have a good record from which to write about our parents' lives.

Now, desiring that our immediate family may know the root from which they have sprung, I have put the story of Lewis (Lew) and Mabel Hern into print, first of all for them.

At the same time, memoirs or biographies of other people's families are very interesting to me. Everyone has parents and relatives who have done a myriad of different and exciting things, if someone has the skill to write it in an attention getting way. When an author can make someone come to life, so that we may feel the pleasures and pain which has dogged their steps, we may want to read it even if these people are not 'my people.' That is my hope here. I dare to hope that this story will remind my readers of the many interesting experiences you have felt within your own family.

May I include a disclaimer for the reader? I ask you to take note of the fact that the author has been a pastor for over fifty years. Perhaps you may pardon the fact that I write from an evangelical Christian perspective which did not reflect the religious leanings of all my relatives, and may not be the mindset of all my readers.

I want to pay tribute to my wife, Sheila, for her patience and perseverance in reading and rereading the manuscript while editing this book for me. Whereas I ask her to 'read for content', the first thing she sees on the page is the glaring error that my typing or spelling or grammar or punctuation has slipped in without my awareness. Interesting that she sees still more of these miscues in second or third reading. I am indebted to her. Thank you, Sheila.

I am also indebted to my brother Gordon for the many helpful memories which he contributed.

II wish I wish I had written before my oldest brother died suddenly. (a story there) No nursing home for him, but a great loss to one who would tell his parents' story.

But most of all, I am indebted to my parents for their contribution to my life and the lives of those for whom they provided **a good heritage.**

Allen Hern June 2020

Table of Contents

Chapter One

Late for my first time

"How did it get so late so soon?
It's night before it's afternoon.
December is here before it's June.
My goodness how the time has flewn."
Dr. Seuss

In the musical "Fiddler on the Roof", Tevye, and Golde have been watching their children fall in love and leave the family nest. This question of love bothered Tevye, and he asks his wife, "Do you love me?"

"Do I what?" me?"

In answer Golde sings "Do I love you? With our daughters getting married and this trouble in our town, - you're upset, you're worn out. Go inside, go lie down. Maybe it's indigestion."

But Tevye persists, "Golde, I'm asking you a question, do you love me?

"You're a fool."

"I know... but do you love me?"

Again, Golde answers, "Do I love you? For twenty-five years, I've washed your clothes, cooked your meals, cleaned your house, given you children, milked the cow. After twenty-five years, why talk of love right now?"

Tevye persists, "Golde, do you love me?"

"I'm your wife."

"I know. But do you love me?"

"Do I love him? For twenty-five years I've lived with him, fought with him, starved with him. Twenty-five years my bed is his. If that's not love, what is?"

"Then you love me?"

"I suppose I do."

"And I suppose I love you too."

Then they both sing, "It doesn't change a thing but even so after twenty-five years it's nice to know."

I think this illustration describes the relationship of Lew and Mabel Hern quite well.

They were my mom and dad and love wasn't something we talked about in our family.

In fact, for many of their generation, love was not a matter of public discussion. The only time I heard my dad say that he loved my mother, she wasn't present. He said it to me, sitting at the Glen Otter railroad station. Dad was obviously needing an understanding ear when he took his teenage son into his confidence, saying, "I love that woman, you know." I wished at that moment that he could have said those words to her rather than to me.

Tevye and Golde's song points up an important truth. Love isn't all starry eyes and soft music. An awful lot of love is "washing your clothes, cooking your meals, cleaning your house, giving you children, milking the cow." A great deal of love is well described in the statement: "For twenty-five years I've lived with him, fought with him, starved with him. Twenty-five years my bed is his. If that's not love, what is?"

You see, as my brother Gordon says, "Coming out of the Great Depression and the Second World War were hard times and it is to the credit of our parents' struggle that our generation were the beneficiaries of their love and care. The poverty of those years scalded them with a fear of indebtedness to the point of caution and alarm when we of the next generation bought a new piece of equipment or anything on credit."

Mom and dad's story really began over 130 years ago, taking us back into the 1800's. Dad was born in 1889 and mom in 1895.

For all of mom and dad's children and grandchildren and great grandchildren, this is a tale that you would never know if we don't get it into print in order that you may know something of your **good heritage.**

It may be that there are others who would like to follow me as I attempt to paint a picture of one family's trials and victories which have prepared the way for this generation.

I am the youngest of three sons born to Lew and Mabel Hern. Mom and dad married in 1924. Their first child, Reba Isabelle, died at birth in 1925. Following that sorrowful experience, Norman was born in 1926, Gordon in 1932, and myself, Allen, in 1939.

You can see at once that I was a latecomer in the Hern household, born when my dad was fifty years old and mom was forty-four so I missed a great deal of their lives.

I joke about the fact that if this pregnancy had been fifty years later, the doctor would have warned mom and dad about the dangers. Certainly, this should excuse all my idiosyncrasies. Hmm, maybe I wasn't late after all.

Fortunately, mom, in her later years, wrote her story and I have those notes. I also have had Gordon as a resource. Being seven years older than myself, his memories reach back farther than mine. I wish my brother Norman was still here to set us both straight but he passed away several years ago.

I first wrote mom's story in 2010, "Á **Life Not Lived In Vain**", sending it out, chapter by chapter on paper or by email to family members and to as many friends as were willing to receive it. That book is still available. I included something of dad, but my sister-in-law, Jane Deyell, has been encouraging me to write dad's story, so with my brother's help, I am starting over, putting together their story, as "**A Good Heritage.**"

As I have indicated, life for people of their generation was hard but there were also life experiences in which they began to enjoy the fruit of their labours. I had the opportunity to observe some of those.

But, having been born in 1939 when the war started, and being six years old when it ended in 'victory', I missed the Great Depression and any real knowledge of the Second World War plus so much more. To set the stage for your understanding, I am going to have to take you back, away back, to see the beginning of your heritage.

Chapter Two

The girl with the auburn hair

"Sometimes you will never know the value of
something, until it becomes a memory."
Dr. Seuss

She stood well back from the banks of the Little Thessalon River, a small, auburn haired girl with her heart in her mouth, watching the cows swim across the river from the neighbour's farm. The year was probably 1901 or '02, two or three years after the family traded a house in Thessalon, Ontario, for a small bush farm in the area called Sherwood, a few miles north of town. Because there was no fence, the cattle would often cross the river to pasture on the neighbour's land, and would have to be driven home again for milking.

Normally the Little Thessalon River was a clear, sandy bottomed and shallow stream which could be waded across quite easily, but these were the days when logging was being carried on in the Kirkwood pine forest, and the logs were dumped into the river to be floated down to the Big Thessalon River and thence to the Dyment Saw Mill at Thessalon. This took place at flood time when the dam at Little Rapids would be opened to provide the extra water needed to carry the logs along, encouraged on their way by river drivers with their long peavies and pike poles to help the logs back into the center of the steam. During those few weeks, the cattle would have to swim among the logs which would be frightening to a little girl.

That auburn-haired girl was my mother, Edith Mabel Rowan Hern. She was your grandmother or great grandmother. On the other hand, she may just be someone of whom you have heard, or someone whom you might be interested to hear about.

Before long, you will also learn something of Lew Hern and their lives together. Like every other couple, they had their joys and sorrows, their stresses and successes.

So here I sit, in February 2020, about to try to capture the lives of Lew and Mabel Hern, in our old stomping grounds of Thessalon, Ontario. Here in Kamloops, B.C. the snow has fallen, and been largely cleared away – a good time to hunker down and write. I hope that you may have an opportunity to hunker down and read.

There's something about being a Rowan:

Mom was the only daughter of Joseph and Isabella (Bella) Rowan from Pembroke, Ontario. She had three brothers, Leonard and Garnet who were older and a younger brother Clarence.

Let me take you back still farther to Ireland in the early 1800's.

According to research by a distant cousin, Gordon C. Rowan, who visited the area in 1967, the Rowan family came from County Armagh in Northern Ireland. From Wikipedia we discover that the Rowan family name comes from the mountain ash tree, and means "getting red."

County Armagh is one of the six counties of Northern Ireland and sits just above the Republic of Ireland. Armagh was not a prosperous land.

"Owing to the political and religious strife of the 16th and 17th centuries, the Irish people were reduced to the position of serfs of alien landlords. Having no security of tenure in their farms, they built the cheapest type of houses. These were often sod-walled cabins without windows or chimneys, roofed with thatch. These dark, smoky hovels had little furniture beyond a bed, a table, stools and an iron pot for cooking. Even as late as 1840, more than a third of the families in towns and half the rural population lived like this to avoid the possibility of a rent increase, or eviction. The farms were small, many less than 10 acres, and all the work was done by hand."

Into this repressed situation, there now came a disastrous experience which History.com describes as the Irish Potato Famine.

"The Irish Potato Famine, also known as the Great Hunger, began in 1845 when a fungus-like organism called Phytophthora infestans (or P. infestans) (potato blight) spread rapidly throughout Ireland. The infestation ruined up to one-half of the potato crop that year, and about three-quarters of the crop over the next seven years. Because the tenant farmers of Ireland—then ruled as a colony of Great Britain—relied heavily on the potato as a source of food, the infestation had a catastrophic impact on Ireland and its population. Before it ended in 1852, the Potato Famine resulted in the death of roughly one million Irish from starvation and related causes, with at least another million forced to leave their homeland as refugees."

Whatever the cause, at least two families of Rowans left Ireland by sailboat to emigrate to Canada in 1831.

James Rowan with his wife and family of five or six children boarded a sailing vessel for the long and difficult trip to Canada. The oldest son, James Junior at twenty years of age had been married just prior to sailing. It appears that during that journey, mother and father and perhaps one or more of the children died of either scurvy or cholera and were buried at sea, leaving young James and Anna, his new bride, in charge of the remainder of the family. Quite a responsibility!

Upon reaching Canada, the young couple came to Pembroke, Ontario, to live on a farm in Alice Township. There they raised a family of 12 children, one of whom was John Rowan who with his wife Nancy brought seven sons and two daughters into the world. One of those boys was Joseph Rowan, mom's father and my grandfather.

I admit that I had never really thought of mom's roots being in Ireland.

Since Grandma Rowan was a McNab from Renfrew, Ontario, I had mostly thought of our family as being of Scots descent.

Grandma Rowan was born Isabella McNab in 1866, one of four daughters of Duncan McNab, a farmer. In the winter he supplemented his income working in a lumber camp.

As mom wrote, "After the fur trade in Canada waned, the timber trade took its place in the economy of the country. Tall and stately pine trees were felled along the Ottawa river and its tributaries, squared with the broad axe, and floated in giant rafts to Quebec City where they were loaded aboard ships bound for Britain.

"Most of the young farmers of those days went to the lumber camps in the winter to supplement their income from their small farms. In camp, each gang was under the supervision of a camp foreman whose first duty was to arrange shelter for both men and beasts.

As lumbermen followed the rivers, communities sprang up along the Ottawa river and its tributaries."

McNab of McNab

Let me swing aside for a moment to give an amusing sidelight to this story.

Archibald McNab was the last Laird of the McNab Clan in Scotland (a title that pleased his vanity).

Calling himself "McNab of McNab", he came to Canada under questionable circumstances.

"In 1822, Archibald McNab fled from his creditors and came to Canada where other members of the Clan McNab had already settled. (Sir Allan Napier McNab, the prime minister of Canada from 1854 – 1856, was his first cousin.)

Striding into the private office of His Excellency, Sir Peregrine Maitland, Lieutenant Governor of Upper Canada, he secured the rights to establish a township to which he gave his own name.

Calling him "The McNab Social Lion", the Ottawa Citizen describes the Laird's appearance as he appeared in Toronto drawing rooms, wearing his full-dress regalia: "the blue bonnet and feather and richly embossed dirk always rendered him conspicuous, as well as the tartan of brilliant hues. A bright scarlet vest with massive silver buttons and dress coat, always jauntily thrown back added to the picturesqueness of his figure."

To McNab Township, he brought Scottish settlers under false pretenses and burdensome terms.

On June 23, 1825, twenty-one families of settlers, totaling eighty four men, women and children landed at what is now Arnprior wharf and were taken to the Laird's house. They had been assured before leaving Scotland that Chief McNab would have a three month's supply of provisions ready on their arrival in the new township. To their utter consternation, they found only a large puncheon of whiskey and a sparse supply of clothes. There was nothing at all in the way of food and shelter.

There was no turning back. They were bound by loyalty to the Chief as well as to their bond "whose terms were very different from those laid down by the Government. The primary purpose was to place the settlers under the Chief's power forever". They were required to sign a bond granting the Laird a mortgage on their lands and "pay to me or to my heirs and successors forever, one bushel of wheat, Indian corn or oats of like value, for every cleared acre upon the said lot of land, in the month of January in each year."

Other immigrants followed, settling upon lands in the neighbourhood of what is now Arnprior.

In 1832, Duncan McNab, (probably one of those early settlers), had the temerity to tell his chief that he did not own the township at all, and that he was nothing more than an agent.

In 1843, this wily old Chief was tried at the Spring Assizes in Perth for being a "public nuisance." This ended all power of the last chief of the Clan McNab.

When those settlers rebelled against his high-handed leadership, he had to leave the country. He died in a fishing village in France at the age of 83 years.

Another Duncan McNab, (probably a son), born in 1831, one of the farmers / lumbermen mentioned above, married Isabel Mackie. They had four children including Jane Isabella McNab.

In 1870, when Duncan was harnessing the horses to leave for home at the end of the forestry season, the barn collapsed, and he was killed. As a result, Grandma lived part of her young life in Pembroke with her uncle, the late Thomas Mackie, a two term Member of Parliament for Renfrew County. Her mother remarried. With John Graham, she had thirteen more children. (Apparently one of her daughters died leaving a set of twins. Isabel took the two children in and raised them. Nineteen children, eh? She must have been quite a woman!)

In October, 1887, at 21 years of age, Isabella (Bella) McNab was joined in matrimony with 22-year-old Joseph Rowan whom we met above.

In November, 1887, following their marriage, the young bride came north by passenger train to Sudbury, then west to Algoma Mills. There, her young husband was employed by his father John Rowan in a camp near the railroad north of Algoma Mills taking out ties for the Sudbury - Sault railroad line. They spent the winter in Algoma Mills.

From that small community, Joe and 'Bella' came by train to Thessalon. The railroad station was then in Sherwood where Morgan's Mill now stands. From the station they were conveyed to the town by bus, using the frozen Thessalon River as a highway.

In Thessalon, Joe attempted for a time to run a taxi and livery business. Apparently, due to a bad business deal, this venture failed.

Always a man to love his heavy horses, Joe Rowan took a team to the Sault where he helped begin the excavation of the Sault Canal. His work there ended when he contracted typhoid fever.

There followed a move to Spragge, Ontario, a small community east of Blind River, where, for three years he worked for the sawmill. Brothers Leonard, and Garnet were born during those years.

An interesting coincidence of this time saw them living in Spragge, near the Lewis Hern Sr. family where Lewis Hern Jr., (my dad) the son of Lewis Hern and Rebecca Spinks, was a boyhood friend of Leonard Rowan.

Following this time, the Rowans came back at last to Thessalon and a home of their own. Interviewed by the 'Thessalon Advocate' over 70 years later, Bella gives this word: "Finally we moved back to Thessalon and I was glad to be there."

There, in 1895, daughter Mabel was born, and later her younger brother, Clarence.

The time in town was not to last. In1899, when Mabel was four years old, they moved to a bush farm, and an unfinished house. A letter from Mom says, "Then my father got the urge to trade our house in town for a bush farm. Hopefully my father would become a farmer, but my mother was not interested in a life such as she would have to live there. She didn't want to make the change.

"There was no quarrelling. My father just seemed to get quiet, and to want to go to the farm. Finally, my mother was the one who made up her mind to let him have his way, and the transfer was made. What a blessed way to give in - no quarrelling or bickering," and she adds, "How I wish I had such a nature!"

The bush farm to which they came was only the centre section of property which later became known as 'the Rowan farm' on 'the Sherwood flats', nestling up against the Little Thessalon River where it met the Big Thessalon River – and so the little girl watched the cows cross the swollen stream among the floating logs as I mentioned earlier.

In the years that followed, Leonard and Garnet worked with their father in clearing land which proved to be very productive. The rich sandy loam soil gave it good drainage and fruitfulness.

Looking back in time:

The world into which Mabel Rowan was born was a very different world than that in which you live today.

In the first place, we are talking about more than 100 years ago. Just think - there have only been 20 centuries since Jesus walked the earth and mom lived through one of those centuries.

As I wrote to her in 1988, when she was 93 years old, "Mom, the greatest thing you can share with your grandchildren and great grandchildren is yourself. They need to know you. You represent over 90 years of history - reaching right back into another century." (In fact, now it is reaching back into the second last century for she was born in 1895.)

"You have known change such as the world never knew prior to your generation. You have done so much in your lifetime. It is a shame that this has not been shared more fully. In your concern for the souls of your family, you have tended to discount your own life, as though there was nothing in your life that would be of interest. Mom, everything is of interest.

"As part of that life there has been the influence of the gospel. Even your weaknesses and failures are important within that story. If only they could know you better - and I am speaking about all of the grandchildren and great grandchildren (and others as well). If they only had known Dad better as well. They know nothing of him - nothing of his hopes and fears."

In fact, she did understand that her story was important, and that is why in her late years of life she began to write it down - in her own handwriting, on 3 ring notepaper. Because she had left it a little too long, she wrote it and wrote it again, not remembering what she had written previously.

She became tremendously interested in tracing the family tree, and wrote to various relatives to get from them the record of the family going right back to Ireland as I wrote about earlier.

She left all of that material to me, and now at last, after 30 years, I am sharing her story and dad's with you.

Just think of some of the changes that took place in mom and dad's lifetime.

For one thing, think of the change in girl's clothing. Girls wore bloomers, and longer dresses. Girls and women's bathing suits were truly 'a covering'. Little connection there to the clothing that girls today are permitted to wear.

There were no electric lights. They read by the light of candles, coal oil lamps, or perhaps Aladdin lamps. Probably that encouraged them to go to bed early.

There was no indoor plumbing. Relief was experienced through trips to the outhouse in the daytime and the chamber pot or pail at night. Even in my early life, the pot or pail had to be carried out and dumped in the outhouse. Oooh, did those things smell! I did it, but it was not a job I relished.

You didn't take a shower every day. Baths were lacking comfort (and possibly privacy, too) in a galvanized tub no more than once a week. Carrying in water and heating it on the wood stove took care of any temptation to waste water.

There was no refrigerator. During the winter, the men 'put up ice'. They travelled out onto the lake, cut huge blocks of ice with ice saws, carried it home by horse and sleigh, and piled it in 'the ice house,' well covered over by lots and lots of sawdust to provide insulation. This was so effective that ice could be kept even through the summer. When you wanted to cool something in the house you sent someone out with an ice pick to chip off the amount you needed. Otherwise, milk and other perishable food could be kept in the ice house when not in use.

Transportation was limited to travel on foot, on horseback, in a horse and buggy, cutter or sleigh. No gas bills, but watch out for the exhaust!

The 'horseless carriage', was just being developed. Henry Ford was just getting his Model A into production and other automobiles were being built in that first decade of the twentieth century. Wikipedia tells me that in 1900 there were only 200 cars in all of Canada, with all of them being in Ontario. Certainly, they would not arrive in Thessalon for quite some years yet.

For greater distances such as travelling from Thessalon to the 'Soo' (Sault Ste., Marie), the train was the way to go.

Entertainment was limited to personal interaction, since the telephone, the radio and the phonograph were just coming into existence around the turn of the century and wouldn't reach an area farmhouse for another 20 or 30 years. Television would not reach the area till well on in the fifties or even later.

Still ahead were two terrible World Wars with the Great Depression sandwiched in between. We probably fail to understand the degree to which those events marked the people of their generation.

Air travel, space travel, computers, and all our modern forms of technology were not even dreamed of when mom was a girl there on the Rowan farm. In fact, Mom and Dad's generation saw more change than any previous age. Their story was important.

Chapter Three

The Family Tree

"We are who we are, because of who they were."

Meet the Hern Family:

y early attempts at 'tracing our family tree' proved to be a 'knotty subject' quickly revealing a variety of roots and branches.

This led to a study of census records from 1851, 1861, 1871, 1881, 1891, 1901, and 1911. Should be a piece of cake, shouldn't it? Ha! You're as naive as I am!

Family names coming from Great Britain and Ireland include Hern, Hearn, Hearne, Hearns, Hurn, Hurne, O'Hearne, and A'Hearne. In the census records of one family of nine children, some were spelled Hern, some Hearn, and a couple spelled Hurn - all in the same list, no doubt due to poor handwriting or an underqualified census taker. But while this in itself can be confusing, in the 1851 census of England and Wales, there are 566 people with the Hern name. I haven't yet been able to match up the ones who came to Canada.

Foolishly perhaps, I could not be content with just tracing our direct ancestors. One naturally looks for connections with others of the same name. My brother Gordon has become good friends with Herns in the Exeter, Ontario area, and I dared to hope that I could discover a family connection which had eluded them to this date.

In the census of Upper Canada in 1851, there were 41 Herns listed. This involved Herns from Ireland, Scotland, and one family plus the two servant girls from England. Their church connections were just as varied, with some identified with the Church of Scotland, some with the Presbyterian Free Church, some with the Church of England, and some with the Roman Catholic Church. One family was listed as belonging to the Apostolic Church.

Now all of this could have set me on a solid trail to discover our early relatives, but after two months of intensive research, I was more puzzled than when I began, since most of the 41 did not appear in the 1861 census, just 10 years later. It's as though a lot of these people just disappeared, due, I am sure, not to their actual disappearance but to the faultiness of my research methods.

None of these Herns were our direct ancestors since my great grandfather did not arrive in Canada till somewhere in the 1850's. He first shows up in the 1861 records.

Here once again I encountered a puzzle. We did not have much information about my grandfather's roots, but we had heard that the family came from Wales.

During their visit to England, brother Gordon and Marge had met Herns who indicated that the family originated in Devonshire. If one examines a map, one can see that Devonshire lies just across the Bristol Channel from Wales, so perhaps this was the answer.

A search of U. K. census records does indeed show that Arscott Hern, the son of James Hern, was born in Devonshire, England, April 28, 1823, married Mary Allin about 1847, and had a number of children, one of whom was Lewis Hern, born in 1853. Ah, here was my grandfather. I was making progress.

Arscott Hern, isn't that an interesting name? Where on earth would that come from as a given name? I'll tell you in a minute.

A description of Devonshire reads as follows: "A County that forms part of the South-West Peninsula of England, Devon is the third largest County and borders the popular Counties of Dorset, Somerset and Cornwall. Devon boasts some of England's finest beaches, has a wealth of interesting history to discover and many pretty villages including Clovelly. Interesting places to visit include Torquay, a popular holiday resort and birthplace of Dame Agatha Christie, the most popular crime writer of all time and Tavistock the centre of a beautiful and fascinating district and birthplace of the famous explorer Sir Francis Drake."

A couple of 'chance' meetings at First Baptist Church in Kamloops, B.C. where I served as associate pastor, was of real interest to me. Within two or three years of each other, two couples came to First Baptist Church for the evening service. One couple was from Devonshire in England, the second from London, England. Both were pastors of Baptist churches. When I shared my possible family connections through an Arscott Hern, each of them informed me that there are numerous Herns in their area, and that they knew one or more of these families. I had always wondered about such a strange first name as Arscott, but they clarified the fact that Arscott is a well-known family name, and that perhaps somewhere in the background a Hern may have married an

Arscott and in that way, the family name came to be used as a given name. Naturally I was excited to meet these couples.

Each of them told me that, after arriving home from Canada, they planned to pass on word of meeting us and see if they could arrange for some connection to be made with Herns in that part of the world. Unfortunately, we never heard from either couple again and my hopes of corresponding with some with our family name did not materialize.

So, what led Arscott Hern and his family to leave England for a very undeveloped Canada? According to writeups about 19th century England there were two main waves of emigration from 'the west country' (including Devonshire), the first being in the 1830's, and a second much larger exodus of about 20,000 people between 1845 - 1854. These dates seem to herald the beginning of a prolonged commercial depression in England that left thousands unemployed or underemployed, so that the emigration net widened into parts of the country previously untouched and dropped markedly down the social scale.

This large number of migrants from the Devonshire area largely settled in York, (now Toronto) Ontario, and Durham counties, along the western half of the Lake Ontario shore between Port Hope and Toronto.

By the 1850s increasing numbers of West Country settlers were also locating to the north in Mariposa Township. This would correspond exactly with Arscott and family settling in Port Perry, northeast of Toronto and north of Oshawa and Whitby. I have yet to find any record of what they did there. Arscott's profession is listed as 'stonecutter'.

When my wife and I lived for three years in Port Perry where I pastored the Port Perry Baptist Church, I was unaware of the family connections that we had with that community.

In light of the fact that dad was born in Port Perry, and dad and mom visited us on more than one occasion, I am especially surprised that nothing was said of the family heritage in that area, though I am sure my dad must have had some knowledge of it.

Though in 1881, there were 18 Herns registered in Port Perry, I was not aware of anyone by that name in 1968 - 71. I did meet one lady who was a relative, but unfortunately, I did not realize the connection, so entirely missed the opportunity to learn more of our family background. Who knows, perhaps I might have found some of his handiwork as a stone mason around the town. I find it interesting too, because here in British Columbia, I have built a good number of stone walls, though not with the skill he would have used if that were his life work.

At any rate, Arscott's family included William, James, Thomas, Albert, Lewis and at least one sister. Of these, James, Thomas and Albert all were said to have moved to B.C. William remained in Port Perry, while my grandfather, Lewis and his new wife Rebecca Spinks, moved north to Algoma Mills, and later to a farm west of Thessalon.

As I mentioned in chapter 2, by a strange coincidence, while the Herns lived in Sprague, (on the north shore of Lake Huron, east of Blind River, Ontario) they lived very close to the family of Joe Rowan. The focus of Sprague was the sawmill. Joe Rowan was a horse man doing mill yard work, while Mr. Hern was a saw filer.

(I said that this was a strange coincidence but are there any true coincidences in human life? Let Desiderata talk about "the universe unfolding as it should" but those who know that there is a living God know better), Is it not a wonder that after the Sprague mill closed, both the Rowans and the Herns relocated to the Thessalon area?

For Grandpa Hern, a sawmill at Nesterville, west of Thessalon, provided employment.

Grandpa Rowan, on the other hand, did not seek a job there but concentrated on developing the farm. Thus, the two families came to live within a few miles of each other in the Thessalon area, the Rowans in a community called Sherwood and the Herns in a community called Alma Heights.

Where did these names Sherwood and Alma Heights come from? From what I can discover, the heights above the Alma River in the Ukraine was the scene of a battle between the French, British and Turkish forces against the Russian army in 1854 in the Crimean War. It is said to have been "a glorious mess of a battle."

However important that was, it gave its name to a small settlement in New Zealand, to Alma, New Brunswick; to Alma, Nova Scotia; to Alma, Ontario; to **Alma**, Quebec and to this farm community in Northern Ontario called Alma Heights. It is also interesting to know that there are Alma Heights Christian schools in California. The name also shows up as the name of churches in California and Florida.

Sherwood is obviously a name that comes from 'the old country'. Sherwood Forest comes to mind, but once again there are Sherwood churches in various places in the United States.

Why Mr. Hern bought a farm is a good question since he was not at all a farmer. His interest lay in the sawmill at Nesterville, leaving the farm work up to his wife Rebecca. and the older children.

At that time, Nesterville was a thriving mill town with company housing, a boarding house, a general store, a post office, poolroom, a Catholic church, and a public school, a far cry from what it became in the years after the mill burned.

With no other employment, it became a small village of older houses.

But a farm it was, located on the Hopper (later Tremelling) sideroad. The farm had a large bush lot and was inclined to be hilly, though with good soil.

"So, what is a woman to do about making a living for a large family? While the boys were growing up, no one was inclined to farm it. Mrs. Hern worked hard to garden and do the best that she could but she couldn't do the work herself.

"A neighbour, Abe Wright, was available, so she hired him at $1.00 a day to take on the job, and being a farmer, things went well for a while. Mrs. Hern and the family were good chore boys and girls. They probably milked about eight cows, had twenty-five or thirty hens, raised chickens and sold eggs. The girls looked after separating the milk, washing the separator and kept the cream in a cool spot in the cellar. It was put into a crock until the crock was full, then brought up into the kitchen where it was left to sour until it was ready for churning. The cream was emptied into a dash churn in which it was dashed up and down until it turned into butter. A later churn was a barrel churn which rolled around and around until the butter was made. They would then wash and mix the butter until all the buttermilk was drained out. What a delicious drink the fresh, sweet buttermilk made and the lovely muffins, cookies and cakes with sour cream or buttermilk were beyond mention.

"Mrs. Hern was a very good butter maker. The butter was salted and made into pound prints with a press to set it firm with an imprint on top of each pound. Then ice was packed around the pounds which were kept in boxes or baskets in the cellar until it was taken to the store. I remember that I once had 65 pounds of butter and a basket of eggs which were exchanged for groceries. The butter provided 15 cents a pound."

To get a fuller picture of life on the farm, a root house was built into the side of the hill, where turnips and potatoes were stored. Eggs were gathered every day from a nearby hen house.

Under the kitchen, the cellar was dug down and shelved to hold the jars of fruit, and pickles and everything that needed to be kept cool.

As we look back to that time, we can see that the growing family was not idle, helping with the farm work. It was a demanding life.

The day came when Abe Wright decided that he wanted a change so Mrs. Hern had to make other arrangements.

Herb did not wish to farm. He was a mechanic and not a farmer. After working at the mill for some years, he found a school teacher to his liking and moved to Sault Ste. Marie where he secured a job in the pulp mill.

But what of dad and the farm? We'll learn more in the next chapter as we follow mom and dad in their early adventures.

So, let's go back now and visit that little auburn - haired girl as she heads out to school in the little red Schoolhouse at Little Rapids, a village north of Thessalon.

She started school at age 7. Her older brothers, Garnet and Leonard, were 12 and 14, and Clarence was just a baby at home. I suspect that most of the time the children walked the 2 or 3 miles to school. She doesn't say so, but I expect her older brothers kept an eye on her until they completed Grade eight. Later, when Clarence was old enough, he walked to school with her and she admits that she bossed him a good deal. I'll bet he loved that!!!

Like all country schools, the little red schoolhouse had all eight grades in one room with one teacher teaching all subjects to every grade level. Each grade was in its own row of desks which were usually made up of 2 parts, a desk of which the front formed the seat on which the student sat up to the desk in front of him. Sometimes those desks were double, holding two children. These desks can be found in the museum at Little Rapids, Ontario or in pictures on the internet under "One Room Schools."

In my experience, those one room schools would have up to 30 or more pupils but mom records a number that was much greater, almost beyond belief. She says that the teachers were often Model School students third class or even just high school pupils, some good, some poor.

Modern day teachers would have no expectation that good education could possibly take place in such a setting, complaining as they do when class size is above 25 in one grade, yet those schools turned out students ready for further education and challenges. The genius of them was that as children sat in their row, they were hearing what was being taught at higher levels. As students went up to work out problems on the blackboard, younger minds were conscious of what was taking place. As each grade lined up in front of the teacher's desk for oral reading class, younger ears were listening, and with it, older students often helped the younger while the teacher was working with a different class.

No doubt it was this training which prepared mom to later become an excellent teacher, mostly serving in one room schools for a large part of her adult life.

Of herself, she says, "I wasn't a brilliant student. I did learn to read and spell well and did well in tables and math, but I wasn't much of a historian or geographical student. I did learn to love grammar, and in my teaching days, I loved to teach literature and grammar. But I was never clever in any way."

Come with me as we watch these two young lives in their early adventures.

Chapter Four

Early Adventures

"Life is a journey that must be travelled,
no matter how bad the roads and accommodations."
Oliver Goldsmith

"If only they could know you better...." This quote from the second segment of Mom and Dad's story was illustrated for me in an unexpected way, when our youngest son responded to a statement about mom becoming a teacher in those one room schools. Darryl said, "I didn't know that Grandma Hern was a teacher."

Of course it is unlikely that he would have, since he was under four years old when we came west to Kamloops, and he saw his grandma only on those rare occasions when we went home for a visit, or when Mom came to visit us in B.C. Mom died when he was 17 years old so he had little opportunity to know her. His comment points up again the reason I want to tell you these stories.

We return once again to that bush farm where Joe Rowan and sons Leonard and Garnet worked at clearing land.

Mom says, "When we were new owners of Lot 22 on the Thessalon River, there were huge stumps on the field around the house. This was virgin timber and these stumps would be very large and probably two or more feet high. My father would start a fire under each and burn them as much as he could. Then Pa, as I called him, would get the horses out with heavy devices and chains, and hitch them to the stump. He always had a good team of heavy horses, and even as a child I was intrigued to see him hitch up the horses, watching as they would pull, pull, pull, time after time until the roots started to give. After several attempts, they would come out. They looked like a huge spider. One after another the stumps would be pulled into a huge heap, and then he'd set fire to them. We didn't fear fire. We didn't even have water handy as I presume he always burned them when the weather was just right."

As mom grew, she shared a special bond with her father. I suspect that she had her father wrapped tightly around her little finger (daughters have a way of doing that to their dads.)

Yet she also reveals the strong-mindedness which was in evidence throughout her life. She tells the following story on herself.

"I needed to get a geography book in Thessalon, several miles away and when I wanted a thing, I wanted it badly and no excuse. It was March and my father got the horse and cutter out to take me. The snow was almost gone, but he drove me to town anyway. We got the Geography book and started home. A bad thunder and lightning storm came up and the rain washed away much of whatever snow was left. Pa walked and drove the horse and cutter which screeched along on the stones while I protected my precious book in my arms as well as I could. He never made any excuse when I needed something and he was always ready to do something for me."

She writes, "I was always somewhat frightened of my father. Yet, as I was the only girl, my father was very protective of me and I was only allowed to go to a neighbour for an hour or so. I didn't always do what I was told, as I sometimes let them persuade me to stay for supper. I remember one Sunday I did this and my father came after me. He really told me off. He had a gad in his hand. He never touched me, but I was always unhappy when he had reason to be cross with me. He was very good to me. He was always very fond of my mother and would often hug and kiss her which I thought was pretty nice to see."

Mom was her daddy's girl and to the end of her life very glad to be a Rowan.

But what of Dad?

I have virtually no knowledge of dad's young life. In notes about his younger sister, Sadie Hern, it is stated that she was born in 1896 shortly after they moved to the farm.

Seven children were in the family: Eva was born in 1885, Della in 1887, Herb in 1888, and Dad (Lewis) Sept. 16, 1889, all in Port Perry, Ontario. Alice was born in 1891, and Grace in 1893, both in Algoma Mills, then Sadie and Effie in 1896 and 1899, both in Thessalon. Thus, dad would have been seven years of age when they arrived at the farm.

Of Grandpa Hern it is said that "he was a very quiet man, of medium height, nice looking and showed all the marks of a real gentleman. He was very straight and upright, brisk of step, with his arms swinging at his sides."

"After moving to the farm, the children went to school at Alma Heights and to Milltown Presbyterian Church, some six to eight miles away. The family were regular attenders and one of Sadie's earliest memories is of a steep hill along the way.

I would imagine that Dad completed Grade eight, but Sadie is the first one whom we know to have gone to High School in Thessalon. More on that, later.

As Gordon says: "Dad was a decent, hardworking person whose education, like many others, was acquired more by life's experience than by formal school training."

Spiritual background:

As anyone should be aware, life is more than just education and hard work. One of the factors that has gotten lost in our present generation with its fixation on sports, and the environment, is that life is also more than physical well-being. Whether people today want to believe it or not, we not only have a mind and a body. We also have a soul, and a spiritual element that is related to the non-physical spirit world. Without attention to this unseen quality, our lives are incomplete.

Before coming to Algoma from Pembroke, mom's mother had been a member of the Regular Baptist Church and her father was part of the Salvation Army. She says, "Both were young Christians but coming to the northern area, they had little opportunity of advancing in their faith. Still, they both clung to the Lord in a thoughtful way, especially my mother in a very quiet observant way, while my father less so."

There was neither a Salvation Army nor a Baptist Church in Thessalon, though a Baptist Church came to town at a later date for a period of time.

There was a Methodist Church and a Presbyterian Church. This was in the days before the amalgamation of the Methodist Church and the Presbyterian Church in 1925 to form the United Church of Canada.

In the Methodist Church, Mr. Lovering was minister. Mom describes him as a very homely man but says he was a good speaker and there she received good gospel messages which she learned to love.

There was a Presbyterian Church up on the hill, and a Presbyterian Church in Little Rapids which she also attended.

"Eventually I got used to the Presbyterian Church and Sunday School at Little Rapids which I could walk to and from. The ministers were dry old country men, not like Mr. Lovering, but we had a lot of nice books such as the Pansy books and others which I poured over delightedly. I loved the gospel messages they contained.

"From 6 or 7 years of age, I always had a deep desire for spiritual things. As I went to Sunday School, we had lovely library books, good gospel stories, and pictures. I loved Jesus Christ from my earliest days. Sad to say, my brothers didn't come to know Him as I did."

A strong influence on her life during these formative years was her Aunt Sis, her father's sister.

"I had an aunt, who joined the Salvation Army in her early years. She never married. In the early years of the Army faith, she suffered much hardship, living in what they called the Barracks and ministering in all kinds of weather. General Booth was the Captain. I do not know how long she served the Army but I know the precious faith this group gave out. Besides the services, they served people in need.

"As Aunt Sis laboured for the Master, her life of hardship began to tell on her and her health broke down. She took tuberculosis and had to come home to her parents, Mr. and Mrs. John Rowan of Sault Ste. Marie, Ont.

"As I look back, I recall the days when Aunt Sis would come to visit at our farm. She had her hammock out under our trees in the warm days. I would sit in my little rocking chair beside her and I would gather pine cones for her to enjoy. As she sat talking to me, all the beautiful Bible stories which Aunt Sis taught me became the basis of my early Christian training, along with my mother's hymns and stories and my father's reading the big Bible at night, especially on Sunday. When she would go back to the Soo, she would write to me in her beautiful handwriting telling lovely stories of my father's sowing the seed in the spring, the growing of the grain and the harvest, comparing it to the great seed time, sowing the seed of God's Word and the great harvest when we would go home to be with Jesus our Saviour- such beautiful messages.

"My father was very fond of this sister and her faith. I can recall his trips to the Soo to see her, knowing she would not recover.

"When she was near the end, Mrs. Carney, a very dear friend, was her constant companion and Aunt Sis made all her funeral arrangements with Mrs. Carney.

"The curtains were to be open with the sun shining in. She was to be dressed in white. Everything was to have the air of cheerfulness. As death faced Aunt Sis, her last words were: 'Meet me there.'

"This touched my father's heart and as a small child, I heard all this. Truly these experiences helped to shape my life."

Dad's family were regular church attenders at the Presbyterian Church in Milltown, later known as Cloudslee.

There at the Presbyterian Church I have no doubt that the messages would be very serious, and doctrinally sound. Emphasis of the preaching would be on understanding the Bible. The 'Sabbath' would be strictly enforced, I am sure.

A bit of humour comes to mind. It seems that a boy had to walk a long way around a lake to attend the Presbyterian

Church. But in the winter, he could take a shortcut by crossing on the ice. He approached one of the 'elders' to ask if he could skate to church? The elders deliberated, and finally told him that he could skate across the ice to church, so long as he didn't enjoy it!

But, joking aside, all through our family's farm years, Sunday was a day of rest. Yes, there were cows to milk, and animals to care for morning and night, but working in the fields and other unnecessary activity was avoided. Church attendance was part of our weekly honouring of the Lord's day, followed or preceded by a Sunday nap. This would have been dad's routine during his growing up years.

I have no idea how strong dad's faith was as a young person but his sister, Sadie, grew up in the same church and remained a strong Christian woman throughout her life. Mom quotes Sadie telling of one of her favourite memories.

Apparently, there was a Baptist minister holding special meetings in the area. Grandpa Hern did not attend. The next afternoon he was splitting wood when the Baptist minister came to the door. He introduced himself and they chatted together. The minister invited Mr. Hern to come to the meeting the next night and, true to his promise, Mr. Hern went. The meeting went well and Mr. Hern became convicted of his sin and 'accepted the Lord,' after which they prayed together. When he got home, though, he was greatly agitated and all he could say was, "I've made a fool of myself."

As the writer of this story, and a Baptist minister, myself, I can understand this situation quite well. As my brother Gordon says, "The Herns were gentle people and Christian faith guided their approach to life."

This was very true of our family. The Presbyterian church, and later its successor, the United Church of Canada, always laid stress upon good moral teaching from the Bible, and seeking to live in a way that will please God. Your faith was not something you talked about. It was a private matter. You didn't talk about sin (although you recited the creed and the confession of sin at the quarterly communion services.) My own experience, though, was that no matter how hard I tried to be honest about my failures at those communion services, I came out of them no different than I went in, having no assurance of my acceptance by God. I think that many people, in whatever denomination they might be, could testify to the same problem.

The Methodist church and the Baptist church, on the other hand, emphasized personal faith entered into by a conversion experience. By nature, every human being has inherited a sin nature, which leads to personal sin in thought, word and deed. Every person from birth is separated from God, incapable of earning God's favour, no matter how good his lifestyle may be.

For that reason, Jesus Christ, God's Son, came from heaven to earth, lived as a perfect sinless human being, and gave His life on the cross to atone for each person's sin and shortcoming.

Through the preaching of the Word of God, a person becomes convicted, and prays to receive Jesus Christ as his or her personal Saviour. If this was led by the Spirit of God, one is "'saved', 'converted' or 'born again.' Although conversion is a one-time experience, producing spiritual life, that life must be nurtured and developed right to the end of physical life.

John 3:36 "He who believes in the Son has everlasting life; and he who does not believe the Son shall not see life, but the wrath of God abides on him."

This initial conviction is what Mr. Hern had undergone. However, being thoroughly grounded in the Presbyterian faith, his experience in that Baptist service led him to feel exposed, and perhaps in some ways, violated.

Daughter Sadie continued in the Presbyterian church throughout her life, but she nevertheless was always so grateful to that Baptist minister for "leading her father to Christ."

Was that true, or was Mr. Hern just as much a true Christian before that experience as after it? I suspect that he was. This difference in basic understanding of Christian faith will show itself again as my mother and father married and lived their lives.

So far as school was concerned, Mom completed her public-school training in the little red schoolhouse, but then what? There were no school buses in those days, and the High School in Thessalon was too far away to reach on foot. The answer required living in town.

Of this experience she writes, "When I started High School in Thessalon I roomed with Sadie Hern at an aunt's home. We brought our own food each Monday morning and went back home Friday night. In the evening, Sadie and I would walk up the street to the garbage dump (now Algoma Manor) and home again for our recreation." How's that for an exciting activity?

She recorded nothing of her actual studies in high school. It's hard for us to conceive the idea of having to room in town during the week when it was just a few miles or so away from home.

There is one more sidelight I want to leave with you before we leave this record of the youthful lives of dad and mom.

Writing about this period of her life, mom wrote, "My parents lived some distance from the Herns, and I didn't know them much until Sadie and I roomed together in Thessalon. Then we got better acquainted, especially with Lew who had his eye on me. I didn't always appreciate his visits to my parents' home. I often was somewhere else when I knew he was coming"

Since dad was six years older than mom, he would already have been about 24 years of age when mom was in her late teens. No sparks there on her part, and some years would pass before dad had another opportunity to try to court the lovely girl with the auburn hair.

So we shall leave these early adventures and pick up the story in the parting of their ways as young adults.

Chapter Five

The parting of the ways

"Sometimes, you have to give up on people.
Not because you don't care but because they don't."
(unknown)

hen I speak of the parting of the ways, it is not as though there were any ways to part.

Although dad may have had amorous feelings toward Mabel Rowan, there is no evidence that those feelings were reciprocated.

Mabel Rowan 'graduated' from Grade 12 in the Thessalon High School, but she, for some reason, had not completed three subjects. Nevertheless, at 20 years of age, she went away to North Bay, Ontario, to take her teacher's training in 1915.

At that time there were two ways to obtain a teacher's certificate. One was through 'Normal School' (the word 'normal' refers to 'according to rule'), providing academic, professional and practical training to students; teaching them educational history and philosophy, teaching methods and classroom organization and management. Teachers graduating from normal school courses would be issued a

First or Second-Class Certificate qualifying them to teach elementary or high school for standard wages. Eventually, it could lead one to become a school principal or school inspector.

The second route was called 'Model School', which was held on the same campus, but was different than Normal School in that they focused on basic practical training and were a less expensive and more accessible method of gaining teacher certification. Students graduating from Model Schools, without also having Normal School training, would be issued temporary **Third-Class Certificates**. This class of certification would permit graduates to teach elementary classes, but would require them to renew their teaching certificate every three years.

This was the course Mom chose, probably because she had not passed geometry, algebra and chemistry. She completed her teacher training and had to teach on a 'letter of permission' until she was nearly ready to retire. Watch for this interesting story of going back to high school much later in this book.

Using the Internet, I have been able to read online the North Bay Normal School Yearbook for 1915 - 1916 where I found her name and her picture. In that year there were 11 students in the Model School and 120 in the Normal School.

It is interesting to look at the pictures of those young adults. First of all, young ladies far outnumber the men. The men are all dressed in full suits with vests, white shirts and ties, and the young ladies all wear blouses and long skirts or long dresses down to the ankles brushing the tops of low boots. No immodesty in 1915!

Since this was the second year of the First World War, it is understandable that the theme of the yearbook is patriotism:

"The Normal School had already given a number of its best to the cause of the Empire. Two of these have since laid down their lives. Still more names were added to the Roll of Honour this year."

There was one other thing which took place during her very short time at the teachers' college which I must include, as it has a bearing on all the rest of her life. Although Mom has recorded that she loved Jesus from a very young girl, she reports that, "As I grew older, I still longed for a Christian life, always going to church and Sunday School. When I went to Model School, I went to the Methodist Church in North Bay, and there, during meetings, I accepted Christ in one of the revival meetings. Yet I was never really sure that I was a Christian. Minnie King, a Christian girl, had a big influence on my life, but I never felt I knew for sure that I was the Lord's. Years later, when a lady asked me if I was saved, my answer was, I don't know. I think I am."

I have spoken of her strong mindedness, but I think this comment reveals that at this point in her life she was confused between the two understandings of Christianity.

Since the Model School was only four months long, while the Normal School was one or two years in length, I am going to include at the end of this chapter a poem someone wrote about those who completed the Model School entrance into teaching.

The poem about Model School graduates.

Farewell to the Modelites
'Tis the week before Christmas,
We ought to be glad,
But for why, can you tell
So many are sad.

We are all going home, hence
You'd think we'd be gay,
With the thoughts of two long weeks
For nothing but play.

But we look round the faces
Familiar ere this,
With a feeling of kinship,
The absent we miss.

This calls up a vision
Of days yet to come,
When again we must gather
To make the place home.

We'll miss your fair faces
Dear Modelite friends,
For your absence, believe me,
Naught can make amends.

And we'll not forget you,
When far, far away
You trudge to your duties,
Each brisk wintry day.

We'll all feel quite certain,
Whatever you do,
You'll honour the Normal
And prove you are true.

The world needs more teachers
As you sure will be;
After all you have picked
From the great knowledge tree.

So our very best wishes
We offer you all;
If you're ever in town,
Don't forget to call.

Now began Mom's real adventures. From Model School, she went to Warren, Ontario where she taught for a year and six months. She makes an interesting comment in her notes. She says, "I really would have preferred to clerk in a store, but a school teacher I became, and again, I am thankful I did."

"Once again I was twitted for my religious feelings and they called me "the teacher with the Methodist feet," because I didn't go to dances and questionable places. I chose to associate with those of similar beliefs. I was especially fond of a young man who was really a third cousin. This friendship grew for some time and when I chose to go west to teach school, he decided to go west also. This friendship was not to my parents' liking and their tears and advice paid off."

You can picture this, can't you? A young couple with strong feelings for one another, but because of being related, unable to secure parents' permission to marry.

But there was another hindrance also. It appears that while mom preferred "those of a more religious nature", there was something that caused mom to hold herself in reserve. It seems that "a more religious nature" was not quite true of Lindsay.

"I felt that if Lindsay would accept the Lord, I would consider marriage on my own. For a time I hoped and prayed for his salvation, but at the end of 5 years, I knew that we would still be 'unequally yoked together' (2 Corinthians 6:14) and it would be best to give him up, and after a year or so he and my dear girl friend were married." While that may have been painful, Mom and Lindsay and Ethel Fraser remained close friends till death separated them.

(This experience points up a problem that will come up again, and be a difficulty throughout her whole life, which I will try to address in a later chapter.)

The question now comes as to what led mom to teach school in Saskatchewan. I have no idea. Her two brothers Leonard and Garnet had both moved west.

Leonard married his childhood sweetheart and took her to the Sylvan Lake area of Alberta where he engaged in farming, lumbering, in heavy equipment and road building throughout his life. Garnet married a girl from Saskatchewan and farmed all his life near Tuxford.

Was it this influence that appealed to a wanderlust in a young woman in war years? I only know that for a year and a half, mom taught in a one room school five miles from Tuxford.

To reach it from Garnet's home, she drove a horse and rig each day. "I could have boarded out at a Blofield home, but I always wanted to get to my own room at night. Later I drove half way with one of the pupils and walked the rest. Finally, I boarded with a man and his nice wife in that community."

This was 1918 and the outbreak of the terrible Spanish or Asian Flu caused her school to be closed.

Once again, I turn to the Internet for information about this disease.

"The **1918 flu pandemic** (the **Spanish Flu**) was an influenza pandemic that spread widely across the world. Most victims were healthy young adults, in contrast to most influenza outbreaks which predominantly affect juvenile, elderly, or weakened patients.

That fall, as our troops returned from WW1, they brought home a silent killer that would afflict one in six Canadians, killing 30,000-50,000 during the winter of 1918.

The pandemic lasted from March 1918 to June 1920, spreading even to the Arctic and remote Pacific islands. An estimated 50 million people, about 3% of the world's population (1.6 billion at the time), died of the disease. 500 million, or 1/3 were infected. Global mortality rate from the 1918/1919 pandemic is not known, but it is estimated that 10% to 20% of those who were infected died. With about a third of the world population infected, this case to fatality ratio means that 3% to 6% of the entire global population died. Influenza may have killed as many as 25 million in its first 25 weeks. This pandemic has been described as "the greatest medical holocaust in history" and may have killed more people than the Black Death.

In fast-progressing cases, mortality was primarily from pneumonia. Even in areas where mortality was low, so many were incapacitated that much of everyday life was hampered. Some communities closed all stores or required customers to leave orders outside. There were reports that the health-care workers could not tend the sick nor the gravediggers bury the dead because they too were ill."

As I write about this pandemic, we are watching in 2020 the outbreak of the Corona virus -Covid 19 in China. As of March, 2020, we are seeing the effects of this pandemic which has affected China, Italy, England, France, Spain and the United States most seriously, but has led to the closure of most public meetings across Canada. As we watch this development, we get a true picture of what 1918 meant to the nations.

How did this affect a young woman far from home and parents?

"I had to take a chance on going home by train when I couldn't get through to my parents to know if they were still alive. Five caskets went on the same train being carried to the east for burial." She also told of caskets piled up on top of one another at the train stations. "Graves couldn't be dug fast enough because of the number of deaths." Internet accounts confirm this.

"Two nuns across the aisle from me kept us all breathing in eucalyptus oil to keep us from getting flu germs. The train was ten minutes late getting into Winnipeg, and I thought I would miss my next train, but the conductor assured me that he would make it up and get me to my next train on time and so I reached the Sault and Thessalon Stations safely to find that my parents were well. I was so thankful after a long tiresome trip."

There followed then a year of teaching at the Little Rapids school she had attended as a girl. Then, her grandfather having died, her grandmother decided she wanted to go west to her daughter. Since she couldn't travel alone, mom once more made the long train journey to Tuxford where she taught for another year and a half.

One other memory comes to mind as mom told us of the fierce dust storms on the prairies, where choking dust could threaten a person in the open. Dust seeped into the houses through every possible crack. This, the constant threat of prairie fires, and raging snow storms in the winter made for an interesting experience.

How easily mom could, like her brothers, have become a 'westerner', and how different her story (and ours) might have been. But after this second period, she returned home to Algoma, and took a position teaching in the Ansonia school a few miles from home. There she boarded with Edna and Donald McPhee, and there Lew Hern once again came calling, with the McPhees urging her towards marriage.

Back to Lew Hern

We started this chapter with the parting of the ways between Lew and Mabel, but now it's time to check back on dad and fill in the gap from his side.

When we last left him, he was a young man on his parents' farm. When Abe Wright no longer wanted to be the hired man it became evident that Herb had no interest in farming. As I have indicated earlier, Herb, with his new bride, got work in the Sault at the Pulp Mill where he eventually became a millwright. Dad didn't want to farm either, but he had older and younger sisters still at home, as well as parents, and someone had to provide for them. With a good deal of dissatisfaction, Lew therefore became a farmer, even though not by his own choice.

In time, Eva, Della and Alice went off to the Sault or elsewhere and Sadie went to Model school just as mom had done. When she returned, she taught at Ansonia for one term, but soon learned that this was not the life for her, so she went to Business College in the Sault and got a job as a secretary at City Hall.

Meanwhile Mrs. Hern (Grandma) had retained control of the farm. Dad worked for some time at the sawmill, while helping his mother.

He built a large barn, 38' x 70', and had considerable livestock and pigs to look after. That barn stood on that property until the Mennonites came into Algoma at the beginning of the 2000s. At that point the barn was torn down and moved to Gordon Lake Road, northeast of Desbarats.

There it was rebuilt in one of their classic barn raisings. It is interesting to watch the whole Mennonite community come together to raise a barn, roof it, and side it in one day. I am sure that is not the way dad originally raised that structure.

As mom says, "Mrs. Hern was a rather bossy woman and things didn't always suit Lew or her either. Further, there was no agreement reached by which Lew could take over the farm."

He did manage to secure a neighbouring farm for himself which sat along Highway 17 and gave the family a mile of frontage on the Hopper sideroad. Bill Tremelling owned the farm on the other side of the road.

We have no record of how or from whom dad purchased that land. My brother remembers that he made payments to one of the neighbouring families for a number of years.

Mom says, "Meanwhile, Mr. Hern, senior, still held his job at the mill until it burned down. From then on, he was always willing to help on the farm. He was never one to show any ill feelings, and at all times was pleasant and understanding. He kept out of financial problems, choosing to spend his evenings comfortably beside the kitchen stove. He was always glad to have neighbours come in for the evening, and while normally quite quiet, on these times his tongue was let loose and he could have the greatest pleasure as they talked over anything and everything of interest and many times Mr. Hern would break out into joyous laughter when something funny came his way."

So, life went on, even for a man who was farming rather reluctantly, but it must have been a lonely life.

Things were about to change. Mabel Rowan had come home, and took the job of teaching in the Ansonia school, just a short distance away.

Mom writes, "Again, after some years of teaching with no permanent certificate, I came, in September, 1922, to the Ansonia school and took on my position of teacher there. I boarded with Edna and Donald McPhee during the winter.

"Again, Lew came around every time I was home. This was his chance and he made the most of it.

"When Lew and I started going together, it was quite clear that his mother resented his attention to me. She had not liked my father, and she resented my seeing more of Lew than she liked. After all, he was her son, and her business manager and the green eyes of jealousy soon became apparent.

"Knowing the early Hern family history, I did not wish to become too involved, but Edna liked and respected Lew and played a good game of matchmaking. Once again, I knew the danger of not making sure of his salvation. Every time we tried to discuss the subject; he would always try to convince me that all was well."

Some good counselling could have helped both mom and dad, but none was available.

"With Edna's counselling, I took the bait and we were married January 16, 1924."

Chapter Six

Joys and Sorrows of Early Married Life

"Marriage is meant to keep people together, not just when things are good, but particularly when they are not. That's why we take marriage vows, not wishes."
Ngina Otiende

o you, Lewis Norman Hern take Edith Mabel Rowan as your lawful wedded wife?"

"Do you, Edith Mabel Rowan take Lewis Norman Hern as your lawful wedded husband?"

Thus, began the married life of Lew and Mabel Hern, Jan. 16, 1924.

The write-up in the Thessalon Advocate read as follows: "The home of Mr. and Mrs. Joe Rowan, Sherwood, was the scene of a very happy event, at high noon, Wed. Jan. 16th when their only daughter, Mabel, was united in the holy bonds of matrimony with Mr. Lewis Norman Hern, son of Mr. and Mrs. L. Hern, Alma Heights by Rev. W.C. Lundy.

"The bride, who was unattended, entered the drawing room on the arm of her father, to the strains of Mendelsohn's wedding march, played by Mrs. George McPhee. The bride was beautifully gowned in navy blue silk and carried a charming bouquet of roses and maiden-hair ferns. The presents were beautiful and costly, showing the high esteem in which the young couple were held.

"After the ceremony, a buffet lunch was served by little Misses Margaret MacLean, Katie Lundy, Bessie Watcher, Catherine and Mable Hopper and Jessie McKenzie, all beautifully dressed in white. The little girls were former pupils of the bride, from her school at Ansonia.

"The happy couple left on the 4:20 train for western points, amid a shower of rice and confetti, the bride travelling in brown velour.

"After the honeymoon, Mr. and Mrs. Hern will reside at Alma Heights.".

Dad was 35 years of age, while Mom was 29.

The question which I am tempted to ask is, "Was this a real love match?" And to that question I cannot give an answer other than that illustration from Fiddler on the Roof.

As I read mom's notes about their marriage, I can't help but feel that she entered into marriage with certain reservations. "Edna liked and respected Lew and played a good game of matchmaking." This is not the best way to start a life relationship.

Long after the fact, mom wrote: "I had hoped that some day I would find one of like faith and marry a preacher - but one never showed up."

Once again, I suggest that this is not the best foundation for marriage. One would hope for a situation in which a young woman finds that this is the man of her dreams, one to whom she can happily surrender her whole heart.

There were spiritual differences which we will explore later. I am sure that dad, when they were married, was a faithful church goer. Mom was, too, but she also had her Methodist background.

At the point of marriage, I believe that mom had other reservations also.

There was Mrs. Hern, Lew's mother. In a former chapter I mentioned that Mrs. Hern looked after the farm with Lew's help, didn't turn it over to her son, and didn't care for this woman whom he now brought into the family.

"When we decided to get married, Lew determined to build a new house for his parents on his new property, which fronted on Highway 17. He and I would take over the old house on the farm. That was okay with me, and we set our date."

Now here was something with which I as the youngest son was completely unaware. I did not realize that dad actually built our house.

My brother Gordon wrote out several pages for me to help me with this story, and he included the fact that, "Dad hauled the gravel for the basement for the new house from the gravel pit in Cloudslee during the winter with horses and sleigh. The pit would have been more than five miles away. It was pick and shovel work as was the mixing of the cement in the summertime." Surely, he must have had a hired man to help him with this very heavy work.

Obviously, this is evidence that this resolution to build a house before mom and dad married was not a spontaneous decision but required a year of planning and building while still carrying on the farm work.

"So, did dad build the house himself, or did he have someone build it for him?" I asked Gordon and he could not answer that question. "Did he have a blueprint or how was the house designed?" His answer was that he had heard that dad used the blueprint from an existing house somewhere in the neighbourhood. Gordon says that although the house was a rectangle, dad had included three-foot eaves which gave the house a quite different appearance, and had been quite pleased with that feature.

Where did the lumber, the windows and all the supplies which were needed come from? I am not sure that there was a local building supply at that time, so it is possible that everything had to be trucked by Fleron Brothers the fifty miles from Sault Ste. Marie. I doubt that anything was easy for that construction.

Apparently, the dwelling remained unfinished, covered with tar paper for many years. Of that I have no memory. I wish I had written this before my brother Norman died, because he would have had more answers to some of these questions.

"The new house wasn't quite finished when Jan. 16, 1924 rolled around." says mom. "When we got back after a week's honeymoon, the curtains in the old house were drawn, and there was anything but a warm homecoming."

Did this new couple need any more stress in their earliest days?

Any newly married couple can bear witness to the time needed for adjustment to this new state of sharing one's life with another human being who has different thoughts and feelings and habits from one's own.

From things mom said to me and yet did not say, I am not sure that their honeymoon had prepared them well for this first phase of their lives together.

Did they live for a while with dad's parents, or did they try to set up housekeeping in the unfinished abode while trying to get it ready for dad's parents to move into?

"When the house was finished after a month, we changed places. Mr. Hern said he was never so happy as when he sat at the big front window looking out the lane at Highway 17, and watched the world go by.

"Mr. Hern was a very fine, kindly man whom I learned to love and respect as my father-in-law.

"Soon after we were married, Lew had not come in to dinner. Mr. Hern was sitting in his favourite spot beside the stove and I was sort of jigging around. Mr. Hern started to laugh and said, 'I believe you could dance if you chose.' I jigged around more than ever and he started to laugh louder than ever. I knew I liked him and it made me feel so good toward him." That's a good picture of Grandpa Hern and of mom who was really a fun-loving person.

"Lew was footing the expense for the new house but he also gave them 2 cows for themselves, while we continued to rent at $25.00 per month, but nothing we did suited Mrs. Hern, especially when I started to remodel the old house and she came over and saw what I was doing."

All of this was part of the joys and sorrows of early married life.

But a far greater sorrow came in the form of pregnancy within the first year.

"A year after we were married, I was pregnant and intended to be at my mother's in Sherwood for the delivery. That didn't happen. Instead I was in the old house at the farm when birth pangs started. I had not had any pre-natal care as we didn't do it in those days and my good doctor who was to look after me was ill and in hospital himself.

"From 5:30 a.m. to 4 p.m. the pain was unbearable. With the country in the grip of a terrible storm, another doctor came by horse and cutter, but couldn't get to Alma Heights before 12 noon. My sister-in -law, Alice Keith, a nurse came down from the Sault, 50 miles away, but couldn't get through on account of the storm until 4:00 in the afternoon."

This was the situation when mom started into labour.

"When he finally arrived, the doctor found it to be a breech case, and without a nurse he was helpless."

This was one time when Mrs. Hern was very helpful.

"My mother got to me, but I didn't want her to see me suffer, and wouldn't let her come into the room. Mrs. Hern, herself not well, held my back and gave me the sympathy I so badly needed in those awful hours. Meanwhile, typical of the day, Lew stayed out at the barn and didn't come in even to see how I was."

"Aunt Alice got here at 4 p.m. and she and the doctor went to work. My dear 9-pound, 10-ounce girl, auburn haired and the image of myself, was finally born but too late. She suffocated with the cord around her neck and her little feet crossed so there was no hope.

"As soon as I knew our little one was gone, I said, 'She was yours to give and yours to take. Thanks be to God.' "

"I was desperately sad but sadder still that I never had another girl."

What were dad's feelings in the loss of this little one? No one has recorded the pain he suffered, nor the attempts he made to comfort his wife. I sincerely wish we knew what happened in those lonely days. No doubt, in typical farm fashion, they just got down to work.

A year and a half after the loss of Reba Isabel, she was pregnant again and this time had the joy of the birth of a little boy. "Along came Norman Rowan Hern, August 3, 1926. While it was a terrible birth, yet the dear Lord spared him and he became quite the young lad - a chatter box who never ceased talking.

"When Norman was born, his grandfather loved him dearly. As he began to talk and run around, Mr. Hern saw how fond he was of the horses. If there was a bridle he could reach, he'd climb the fence until he could get to it and he'd have it on his head in no time at all." This love for horses continued through his life – a throwback to Grandpa Rowan. Indeed in many ways, Norm was more of a Rowan than a Hern throughout his life.

The relationship with Mrs. Hern did not improve. "One day Lew said to me, 'Mabe, you don't need to keep the peace any longer. Mother has continued to find fault with you and I'm not going to expect you to keep on.'"

With that, mom determined that she was leaving the old house and they could come back to it.

The two couples changed places, with Mr. and Mrs. Hern going back to the old house, and mom and dad moving to the new house on Highway 17. "I did everything I could to see that her house was in order and was rewarded when she said I had really made the old house so nice."

"For the next two years I stayed at home, while Lew kept on working the farms. Then I think I must have had a premonition. It was Christmas Day. We had gone down to my mother's for dinner. That night I said, 'Lew, let's go over to the other place tonight.' They were so surprised but we had a pleasant evening and once again we were congenial."

That improved relationship proved beneficial for the following July, (1929) brought the sudden and unexpected death of Mr. Hern.

"July came and haying was on and how thankful I have always been for that reconciliation, especially for Mr. Hern's sake.

"Grandpa Hern was always ready to help. He wasn't a good horseman, and it was fun to watch him driving the horses. He held the lines up high and chirped away at them. One night he put the horses out to pasture, and had a good evening visiting with a grandson who had come to visit. About 4 o'clock the next morning, we were awakened with the news that Mr. Hern was very ill.

"We rushed over to find him unconscious. We got the doctor as fast as we could, but he was in a coma from which he didn't recover. Alice got to him as quickly as she could and nursed him patiently but he passed away at the end of a week.

"What a sad time it was. The whole family was there, and I must say, I was a sad daughter-in-law."

Part of the obituary in the paper reads, "The deceased was a kind and loving husband and father, a good neighbour and was held in high esteem by all who knew him.

"He leaves to mourn his loss his wife, two sons, Lewis of Alma Heights, Herbert of the Sault; five daughters, Mrs. George Fletcher, Rosemont, Mrs. D.W. Giffin, Sarnia, Mrs. Percy Runnalls, Barrie Island, and Mrs. L.S. Keith and Sadie of the Sault; one sister, Mrs. Wm Tremeer, Toronto; four brothers, William of Port Perry, James of Vancouver, and Thomas and Albert of Sayward, B.C."

As well as this sorrow, 1929 brought on that terrible time known as 'The Great Depression.'

Almost unknown to today's generation, it began with the enormous 1928 wheat crop crash followed in 1929 by the Wall Street Stock Market Crash. It was said by the Federal Department of Labor that a family needed between $1200.00 and $1500.00 a year to maintain the 'minimum standard of decency.' At that time, 60% of men and 82% of women made less than $1000 a year. Can we today imagine such a low income?

Prices plummeted and wages dropped even faster. This depression affected everyone in some way and there was basically no way to escape it. Relief programs and work camps for single men did not alleviate the need. It was estimated back in the thirties that 33% of Canada's Gross National Income came from exports; so the country was greatly affected by the collapse of world trade. The four western prairie provinces were almost completely dependent on the export of wheat. The little money that they brought in for their wheat did not cover production costs, let alone farm taxes, depreciation and interest on the debts that farmers were building up. The net farm income fell from $417 million in 1929 to $109 million in 1933.

Farmers did anything possible to try to support their families. Our family was fortunate to own a bush lot, an elevated bluff that was landlocked. Still, it cornered onto the original Hern property. It was only accessible in winter, because the corner connection was through a swamp. When there was enough snow for sleighing, dad, and later dad and Norman would take the team and sleigh back there to break the trail, to let the frost into the swamp. That initial trip was hard on men and horses, and they would come home wet and exhausted.

Before Norm was old enough, Dad had a contract with the Thessalon School Board to supply firewood to town schools. Those were days when jobs were scarce and men could be hired for $1.00 a day and board. Men were hired to cut hardwood up in that remote area. Maple trees were cut down, cut into 30-inch lengths with crosscut saws, and then split and piled for drying. I imagine that swede saws were already in use as well.

As Gordon says, a lot of weight could be moved with a team and sleigh, especially if the road is level or a little bit downhill. The sleigh was loaded, probably with last winter's wood and hauled down to what was called the Scheurman road, across the CPR tracks at the eastern end of Nesterville, then down Highway 17 to Thessalon. Gordon says that was probably 1932, '33 or '34. Work in those days was over unplowed roads and facing the weather, regardless of the temperature.

Could a person make a living from the farm? Mom reports that prices were poor. Cattle were a cheat on the market. "We had a dozen lovely fat steers about 3 years old. When we tried to sell them, Alf Shaw the butcher offered Lew $12.00 a piece. Lew said he couldn't sell them for that. Lew said he'd put on a meat rig, and sell them wherever he could. Mr. Shaw said, 'Do whatever you have to, Lew. I can't give you a bit more.'

"So, within a short time, we were in the meat business. Although Lew was a novice in butchering, he killed our own animals and sold them on the market, cutting, wrapping and delivering the orders each morning to town. Norman was now perhaps 6 or 7, so on Saturday, he delivered the meat to town with his dad. He was a great little chatter box and people liked him. One African lady who bought meat gave him a lovely card which said, "I have a box of soldier boys, I like them best of all my toys. They're made of wood and are so good, they never fight or make a noise.' He was so proud of that card.

"In addition to the meat, we bottled and sold milk to customers. At times we would be up till 2 a.m. in preparation for the next morning.

"Later we bought out a second milk business and then a third. Even at eight cents a quart, we were able to keep our home intact after several years of business. While we didn't make a fortune, we managed to keep our business alive and thriving and so we got by.

"By this time, it was completely a milk business and just when we were well on our way, the pasteurizing law came into force, and as we couldn't afford to take over the pasteurizing plant, in a short time we were out of the raw milk business."

The joys and sorrows of early married life.

Two little stories from that period help to give a picture of my dad and the integrity which was such a vital part of his life, and of the heritage he passed on to us boys growing up in mom and dad's home.

To be prepared for the next day, our parents spent the evenings cutting and wrapping meat. On one of those occasions, dad cut his hand so he had to call on a neighbour who was also selling meat. While Jim was cutting and talking to our parents, he held up a nice roast of meat and said, "Isn't that a nice-looking roast, Lew?" Dad hesitated for a moment and then said, "Jim, there's a knuckle as big as my fist in the centre of that roast." Jim grinned and said, "Yes, but just don't give one to the same customer twice." Dad didn't use him again.

As I heard it, with things so financially difficult as was the case with all the farmers in Algoma, dad went in one day to the bank manager to tell him that he could not afford the monthly payments on the farm. Apparently, the manager said to him," Lew, you are having trouble meeting your payment and you come and tell me about it. The people I have difficulty with are the ones who cross the street, rather than meeting me, and pretend that everything is alright." The manager carried dad until he could catch up with the shortfall. That integrity was passed on to each of us three children with good benefit.

While there was no doubt satisfaction in working so hard to achieve a life together, in later life, mom looked back on her marriage with sadness.

"I am not trying to hold myself up as the Christian I had hoped to be when I got married. The happy home I had envisioned turned out to be anything but, and I assure you, Lew was not always to blame. I myself was anything but the spiritually minded wife I had started out to be. While I taught Sunday School, and went to church regularly, I was not a happy Christian."

As I said earlier, the differing opinions about what constitutes real Christianity no doubt revealed themselves in their relationship. Christian faith certainly doesn't make a person perfect, and greater humility and acceptance of one another's outlook would probably have eased at least that part of their early married experience.

We leave them then, still in the midst of the great depression but solvent and hoping for better times and better days.

Chapter Seven

Blessings and Trials
of Middle Age

"There are blessings hidden in every trial in life, but
you have to be willing to open your heart to see them."
Anonymous

M y wife Sheila and I were sitting together about the
time of my turning 40 and I joked to her, "Don't
say anything bad about middle age. It's looking
better all the time!"

That was only yesterday, 41 years ago. Where did middle
age go?

Well, so it was also with dad and mom.

We have already seen the joys and sorrows of early
married life, which included the stillbirth of their firstborn
child, a beautiful auburn-haired girl. I'm sure that the loss
of Reba Isabel left a continuing sorrow in the hearts of both
mom and dad.

That heartbreak must have been eased to some degree
through the birth of Norman a year and a half later. How

thankful they must have been for his exuberant spirit which also delighted Mr. Hern, senior. Yet in just over three years, Mr. Hern died suddenly in 1929 and the country and the world was plunged into the Great Depression which lasted all through the thirties to be followed within a few short years by the Second World War.

After Grandpa Hern died, Grandma went to the Sault to live with Aunt Sadie, one of dad's younger sisters. It is worth taking a moment to look at a sidelight of Grandma's move.

Aunt Sadie, whose proper name was Sarah, never married but spent her working life as a clerk for the City of Sault St. Marie. She had a house on Albert Street and there, in addition to her work at City hall and her constant teaching of children's Bible Clubs, she looked after her mother until Mrs. Hern's death in 1957. Twenty - eight years!

Neither Gordon nor I have very clear memories of Grandma Hern. My impression is that she was a rather sharp-tongued person who "ruled the roost." Perhaps this is an unfair assessment, but I have always associated an angular body type, a high-pitched voice and a high-strung nature in each of my aunts as a 'Spinks' trait rather than a Hern characteristic. Dad, too, had something of that high-strung nature, whereas my Uncle Herb appeared in looks and temperament to be more like Mr. Hern as he is pictured by Aunt Sadie and my mom.

At some point after Mrs. Hern's death, Sadie took her widowed oldest sister into the home and did it all again. Aunt Eva in time also suffered from dementia but was never put in a nursing home. Over and over Sadie would be asked the same question and time without end she would answer. By the time Aunt Eva passed away, Aunt Sadie herself was worn out and she needed to enter Algoma Manor - one of our unsung heroines.

But, let's go back to the depression times which played such a strong part in the lives of those days. We read that as the depression carried on, one in five Canadians became dependent on government relief. 30% of the labour force was unemployed, whereas the unemployment rate had previously never dropped below 12%. We read of the men 'riding the rail' which referred to men hitching a ride in boxcars on the railroad without paying a fare as they travelled across country to one of the cities, seeking employment which was almost non-existent. We have heard also about men coming to the door seeking a handout, offering to work just to get some food. I don't think any of us who did not live through 'the dirty thirties' can fully appreciate the effect that time of deprivation had on those who lived through it.

But while life was hard, it wasn't all bad. In 1932, nearing the height of the depression, mom and dad welcomed another child into the family. Norm said that when the baby was about to be born, he was sent to the Rowan farm to be looked after by Grandpa and Grandma Rowan.

He came back to find a red headed little brother whom they named Gordon Herbert. From the beginning, Gordon had beautiful copper coloured hair which I always admired.

Because of the challenges of keeping up the farm and the meat and milk business, a girl named Ida Warnock came to live with them for three years to help look after Gordon. Mom relates how Ida loved the little boy whom she called by the nickname "Gudgie".

Gordon was a much quieter and more introverted boy than his older brother. With 5 ½ years between them, Norman remembered that Gordon always seemed to have ability to make things with his hands. One such item apparently was a little wagon. Norm also felt that Gordon always had an interest in music. Though I am not sure how long Gordon took piano lessons, his ability to play the piano, the old pump organ, the accordion and the keyboard by ear has continued throughout his life. Especially in later years this gift has brought a great deal of pleasure to both Marge and Gordon, and to many others. For some years the "Friends and Neighbours" band entertained in nursing homes and other settings, and since that broke up Gordon and Marge have been 'on the go' to various music venues where he is always willing to participate in toe tapping music.

We have already heard how dad began to butcher cattle and learned to cut and wrap meat and peddle it to the doors of customers in Thessalon. After some time, they were also bottling milk, and delivering it to the door in town and in this way, they may have kept the wolf from the door better than many others.

I can only imagine the work involved.

Gordon says, "My earliest memories start with our older brother Norman's interest in the farm animals. The result was that Norm learned to work hard from a very early age."

Of Gordon, himself, he remembers that dad often held him on his knee, even while smoking his pipe. That is a pleasant memory.

The barn in which the cows were milked was a mile away from our farm house (back what was called the Hopper or Tremelling side road), so dad would be up at 5:00 a.m. to put on a fire in the kitchen stove, have breakfast and get to the barn to do the milking. Then back home to load the packages of meat and/or milk into the 1927 Chev car for delivery in the town which was five miles away. I don't know how often delivery was made but I'm sure it had to be no more than 2 or 3 days a week, since there was all the regular farm work of plowing, seeding, haying and harvesting.

When there were cattle or pigs to be slaughtered, I think that would have been done in the upper part of the barn on what we called the barn floor. The carcasses would then be hung from a beam to cool and to cure, until they were taken to the cutting room to be cut up and wrapped. Dad learned how to make sausage using a specially adapted meat grinder that fed the blended and seasoned sausage meat into endless sausage tubes. There was quite a knack to twisting the filled tube into 6-inch lengths then tying them back into clusters of half a dozen or so sausages ready for wrapping. When I was a young fellow, dad resurrected the meat grinder and started making sausage again just for our family and I can testify that they were very good. I remember him seeking and finding 'white pepper' to give them their distinctive flavour.

For most of the time dad would have to have a hired man to help with the work. When Norman got old enough to walk across the fields to the Alma Heights school, he would come home, change and go to the barn to help with the evening chores. "Not in the morning," he says. "Just in the evening."

Mom often told of how in the evening she would go to the door to see if there was any sign of Dad and Norman and the hired man coming home from evening chores. In the distance, she would hear Norman, the chatterbox, talking away to dad as they made their way home for supper. She carried that memory into her late years.

But middle age wasn't easy. Electricity did not come to the farm until on in the forties so mom did her washing in a wringer washer powered by a gasoline engine. While this was a step up from a wash board in a tub, that gas motor proved to be a temperamental beast.

On wash day, dad would get the engine started for her before he went off to the farm but often it would quit on her and she always had difficulty getting it started again. I suspect that many were the tears of frustration on washday.

After being washed, the clothes went into a rinse tub before being put through the wringer and into the basket to be taken to the line.

Some of my readers will remember the white things going into a wash tub in which "bluing" was put into the water to get the white clothes white, after which they were put through the wringer again. The clothes, when they were washed, were hung on the outside clothes line to dry, in fair weather or foul. Do some of my readers remember the clothes freezing on the line in the winter before they were dry, then being brought into the house as stiff as boards? After being brought in from the line, much of the clothing and sheets had to be ironed using what was called a "flat iron" heated on the wood stove. Do you remember how you tested to see if the iron was hot enough? A little saliva was put on the finger which was then tapped quickly onto the bottom of the iron. If it "snapped," the iron was ready for use. If not, it had to be heated more.

In our present day of automatic washers and dryers, and permanent pressed clothing, life has become quite a lot easier but I am thankful to retain one aspect of those earlier days. At the home which we have just sold after 11 years, there was a pulley clothes line on which my wife hung the wash to dry when the weather was suitable. Electric dryers are great but they don't produce the fresh smell of clothes dried on the line.

As I indicated in the last chapter, the meat business gave way to selling bottled milk in town but in 1938, a law was passed in Ontario outlawing the sale of unpasteurized milk and since mom and dad could not afford the pasteurizing equipment their milk business came to an end.

Apparently, there was a flood of interest in getting a licence to operate a dairy, to the point of having to call in a mediator to a meeting at Bruce Station. Animosity rose to the surface, with no conclusion. Dad offered the mediator an invitation to supper with the promise that he would help him catch the evening train back to Sudbury. Gordon claims that this man asked dad "What do you think I should do about this deadlock?" Dad replied, "Due to the hostile nature of those present, give them all a licence and let the cards fall where they may."

In these early years before electricity came to the farm, the cows were milked by hand. Gordon says, "Dad smoked a pipe as long as I can remember, and even smoked it while sitting on a stool milking the cows." Of course, since the pipe was always going out and needing to be relit, I suspect that the cows were in little danger.

As the years went by, first Norman, and then Gordon helped with the milking.

The milk was put through a strainer and kept in eight-gallon milk cans. To keep the milk cool, dad cribbed in a cold spring in which the cans of milk were kept.

Gordon says that, "As a boy, I remember when the family brought firewood out of the bush in four-foot lengths or even as long poles and it was piled to await the spring wood cutting bee. A buzz saw and engine, (later, a tractor), was taken from farm to farm and the neighbours exchanged work.

"In later years, Norm and I were in the bush cutting and delivering firewood to our local public school and there was a trend toward buying chain saws, so we went to town and purchased a power saw between us and that became a learning experience. The motor was temperamental, and the chain would break, so we always had to have teeth and rivets to fix it on the spot.

We often had trouble with it cutting butter bowls because of improper filing which caused the blade to bind and exasperate us. For a long time, Dad wouldn't interfere, but he was aware of our problems, and finally he said, "Give me that saw and let me see what I can do with it". Because he understood the principle of keeping cutting teeth equal and even, and the raker teeth filed to a sort of formula, in short order he had the saw cutting the way it was meant to cut.

The years rolled along and in 1938 mom found herself pregnant once more. I have never learned whether I was "planned" or an "accident", but I have often joked that since mom was now 44 years of age, and dad was 50, today's doctors might have warned them about "possible complications", so therefore I have an excuse for all of my idiosyncrasies!

I was the only one of my siblings to be born in the hospital. Dr. Grigg insisted on it despite mom's protests about hard times. Mom reports that she was in good condition and I believe that this time she delivered more easily.

Was she at last to get her little girl? No! Another boy, but a friend, Mrs. Harris Feagan came to see her and said, "Maybe he'll be your minister." Mom says, "I had never expressed the desire for a minister, but I had secretly hoped that though I might never be a minister's wife, I might be a minister's mother."

So begins the story of Allen Garnet Hern.

As you have seen, I was a latecomer in the Hern household, but I arrived in time for two notable improvements in farm life.

One was the coming of electricity to the farm in the mid forties. That allowed a milking machine to be added plus an electric water-cooled milk tank. The second was the purchase of the first tractor, a Massey Harris # 20. Gordon thinks that it probably cost about $1500.00. Then came the purchase of a two-furrow plow, and other machinery to go with it. Both of those improvements made a great difference on the farm. As Gordon says, "the acquisition of power machinery during those years was part of the evolution and change that happened during dad's lifetime as everything began to expand into the future."

For many years, the hay was cut with a six-foot mower, pulled by horses. Now that gave way to the tractor. The cut hay was then piled into windrows, first with a dump rake, later by a side rake. When dry, the horses were hitched to the wagon, pulling the hay-loader which picked up the windrow and carried the hay up to be deposited on the wagon where a man was busy forking it out as the load was built before being taken to the barn.

That barn that dad built had a track high up in the peak which carried a hay fork that was brought down and driven into the load to pick up bundles of hay. A horse was attached to the cable which ran through pulleys on the hayfork and on the carriage high above. When ready the bundle was pulled up to the track and carried along until tripped over the place where it was needed. Dad or one of the boys would than spread it out around the mow, sprinkling it with loose salt to preserve it. Hot, dry, dusty work from which one would come down, drenched in sweat. I was never really a part of that operation.

I do have the joy of remembering the threshing crews. In those days, before combines came into being, our neighbour, Jim Tremelling, had the only threshing machine in our area, taking it from farm to farm. On threshing day, all the neighbouring farmers brought their horses and wagons to load the stooks of grain. With one man on the wagon to place the sheaves and tramp them into place, several other men were on the ground lifting the sheaves with their forks to throw them up onto the load. The driver and one other man then drove the horses and wagon to the barn, pulling in beside the machine. The sheaves were forked one at a time onto the apron which drew them into the beaters. The grain was blown through the pipes into the granary while the straw was blown onto a straw stack.

When I was young, my job was to stand in the granary to shovel the grain back from the spout into the bin and keep the pipe from clogging. That was hard, itchy work but it meant that I was 'one of the men', and got to sit with them at the tables loaded with food at meal time. Oh, how the men ate, not only the first course, but the pies! I think it was rare for a man to have only one piece of pie.

As the fields were cleaned off on each farm, the machine moved on to the next farm and the process was repeated. Good days!

For a while dad sold milk to Bilodeau's dairy in Thessalon, but in a few years, local dairy farmers were shipping their milk to Harrington's Dairy in Sault St. Marie.

When there were several full cans, they were taken by horse and buggy to the Glen Otter railroad station where the cans were loaded unto the train. The empty cans came back on the same train. One of the social enjoyments of the farmers was meeting at the loading platform. Between the gossip exchanged at the station, and the ladies being able to listen in on the telephone party line, the community kept abreast of the latest events.

Do you remember the telephone boxes on the wall with a hand crank with which you used to give one long ring to get the operator or a combination of long and short rings to get your neighbour? A party line meant that a number of neighbours shared the same line. The receiver could be gently lifted to hear other people's conversation. There was nothing malicious about this. It was just a good way to keep up on the goings on in the neighbourhood. The joke was that one could often tell which neighbour was listening in by the sound of breathing into the phone or other identifiers. But if there was ever an emergency, one long extended ring would bring the neighbours to help put out a fire or whatever the need was.

After Bell Canada bought out the local telephone companies in later years, our neighbour Bill Tremelling, complained that it was a sad day when a fellow had to read the newspaper to find out what was happening to the next-door neighbour!

In those earlier days, houses were illuminated by coal oil lamps, Aladdin lamps, or sometimes by candles. The light in the barn was supplied by coal oil lanterns hung on posts. The farmers were always so careful with those lanterns that barn fires were almost unheard of.

As was the case in so many farming neighbourhoods, at the centre of the community was the one room school and the local church.

In 1962, our local congregation celebrated the 60th anniversary of the little white church on the hill which was the Alma Heights United Church. In the anniversary booklet, a former and long serving minister of the congregation inserted the following poem.

The little church of my childhood
Has changed with the passing years;
It has carried our joys and our sorrows
And has been baptized with our tears.
Moved from its early location
To a lower and easier bed
And clothed with paint and varnish
Still raises its pious head.
To lead our hopes of tomorrow
From a rich and fertile sod,
Towards that eternal City,
Whose Builder and Maker is God.
Rev. R. W Beveridge.

The presiding minister, Dr. James Semple, included the words of W. E. Gladstone, British statesman and Liberal politician who served for 12 years as Prime Minister of the United Kingdom. Dr. Gladstone said, *"Discard the Scriptures and all you have left is a scaffold on which to hang civilization."* How I wish that the present leaders of our country had that kind of understanding of Canadian and world conditions.

All the children attended the community school and all the farm families in our area attended the community church. Each family had their own pew. We sat about the middle on the right side. Ahead of us were Elmer and Grace Campbell and their children, then Jack and Wilma Dunn. Behind us sat Bill and Pearl Tremelling. Across the aisle were the Horricks, the Prouds, Cecil and Annie Campbell and others. The back pew was reserved for the single fellows of whatever age.

There was a real homey feeling about that congregation. Bill Tremelling used to rumple my hair and call me "Butch." We belonged.

Church was held at 3:30 in the afternoon because this was a "four-point charge". Zion United in Thessalon got the eleven o-clock service. Livingstone Creek got the early afternoon and then the minister hurried off to Alma Heights United Church. I believe that the fourth point was the church at Little Rapids. Because he was always in a hurry, we called him "the sky pilot". The farmers in Alma Heights who were up early to do the chores had a rest after lunch and, by the time we were seated in our pews, I felt sorry for the preacher because the men often tended to doze off in the pew during his message.

After the church service, the women and younger children had Sunday School. For many years, mom taught the Adult Sunday School class. This was a women's class as all the men and boys, as soon as we were old enough, went out and sat in the cars swapping stories and 'chewing the fat', until Sunday School was finished.

As a small child, I was part of this church going family. From my earliest days I was in the pew with my parents. I was also in Sunday School where the teachers taught us from the Bible, using story pictures, and Bible verses on little cards.

When I sat with mom and dad in our church pew in Alma Heights United Church, I watched my dad every Sunday bow his head on his hands on the back of the pew in front of him. To my mind he was praying to God before the service began.

Through those years I would sometimes see him on his knees beside his bed. There was no doubt in my mind that he was praying. At the same time, he was not someone who would talk about his Christian faith (or lack of it for that matter.) Nor would any of the other farmers who attended the Alma Heights United Church.

A couple of godly aunts gave me subscriptions to Power magazine and other Christian materials, which I eagerly read. I believe that my heart was very tender toward the things of God and I can truthfully say that "I believed" in God and Jesus. In fact, I believed everything in the Bible. I believed in God. I believed that He sent His Son from heaven. I believed that Jesus died on the cross for my sins. I believed that He rose again from the dead, and ascended back into heaven. I believed that Jesus is coming to earth again to bring all things to their climax and completion, judging those who do not believe and rewarding those who are true Christians.

I was a "believer".

And what was true of me, I believe was true of dad. Like me, I am sure he believed everything in the Bible, though I don't remember him reading the Bible for himself.

From a young age, the idea was always in my mind that I might become a minister. One might wonder upon hearing this, if the desire to become a minister or pastor was instilled in me by a mother's suggestion or by certain pushing. I have no memory of mom ever suggesting such a thing to me, but for some reason, I did feel that I would one day be a minister even from childhood. Now, after spending a lifetime as a pastor, I can look back on that childhood interest with wonder.

Yes, we were a church-going family and a church-going community.

But is just going to church and believing the teaching of the Bible enough?

I 'joined the church' when I was twelve years old, but I don't remember anyone asking me if I had received Jesus into my life.

As I entered my teen years, I had all the struggles with sin and sinful thoughts that are normal for a young fellow. That led to guilt which caused me to question my Christian faith. I have already related the fact that the quarterly communion services did nothing for me. I tried most earnestly to confess my sins, and ask for forgiveness. Yet this prescribed religious act did not satisfy any real need of my heart or soul.

The Bible says in John 1:10 *"He (Jesus) was in the world, and the world was made through Him, and the world did not know Him. 11 He came to His own, and His own did not receive Him.12 But as many as received Him, to them He gave the right to become children of God, to those who believe in His name: 13 who were born, not of blood, nor of the will of the flesh, nor of the will of man, but of God."*

The Bible makes clear that there is "believing" but also "receiving" and that this is not a denominational distinctive, but "the will of God." Yet I am not sure that this need of personal faith was made clear.

I have no idea if dad had any of these same feelings of deep inability to please God by his own good deeds. I do remember him telling me once that he felt unworthy to be an elder in the church. Yet, talk of "assurance of salvation" probably sounded presumptuous.

The home into which I was born was not without its share of tensions. Not everyone will appreciate my references to religion or religious differences. Nor would everyone understand what I was meaning or why I would choose to mention it. But I am writing this story, first of all for those of you who are grandchildren or great grandchildren and I want to help you to know your grandpa and grandma as they were.

As Norman says, "Mom was a good woman, a good living woman." and I would agree. It is helpful to remember that when I referred to Mom "not being the Christian I had hoped to be when I was married," that is not a negative assessment on my part but it is her assessment, written in her journal in later life. There were areas in which she wished she had done better. I think most of us can identify with that.

In those days, a great deal of family life was lived in the kitchen. That's where the cookstove was with its desirable warmth.

Brother Norman, with his love of horses, would order a side of leather from the catalogue, cutting the leather into strips, in order to make his own harness. Punching holes with an awl, he would sew the leather with a heavy needle and multiple ply thread, waxed to give it strength and durability. To do this work he sat on a four legged 'harness horse' (I have no idea what else to call it). Ahead of the seat, a pair of wooden jaws could be closed with a foot lever to hold the leather in place while it was being worked on. That leather was oiled and worked to make it pliable, and so new harness was made or used harness was repaired. Where better to do this than in the kitchen in the evening while listening to the radio. It made for a variety of interesting odours.

In that same kitchen, dad would sit and smoke his pipe or sometimes smoke cigars. Sometimes visitors were also present with their cigarettes or stogies.

Dad also sat in that kitchen filing our saws, whether a hand saw, a Swede saw or a cross-cut saw. You can see that the kitchen in those farm houses needed to be large. It was the hub of the whole operation. I'm not sure how mom got all her cooking and baking done at the same time.

Between the smoking and the kitchen woodstove, the painted kitchen walls had to be washed down every summer. There was a compound that felt something like plasticine that could be worked into a hand ball which was used to rub down the walls, turning it in and squeezing it to get a fresh surface for further rubbing. That compound would pick up the layered smoke. As it was rubbed over the walls, its colour changed from pink to black then back again as it was folded into itself. It did the trick and the walls could then be washed and perhaps even repainted. One was always surprised to see the bright colours again emerging.

Heat in the rest of the house came from a wood furnace in the basement which sent its heat up through a four-foot square register in the floor. The centre was a round grill from which the heat came. Outside that circle was the cold air register, by which the cold air was drawn off to provide oxygen for the fire. Heat for the second floor was provided by a one-foot square grill in the ceiling over the register. Since us boys slept up there, I can testify that it certainly did not get overheated. In the winter time, we would often spread our long underwear between the sheet and the blankets so they would be warm when we crawled out into the cold to get dressed. Body heat can be quite efficient.

A year and a half after I was born, mom was offered the opportunity to teach in the one room school at Nesterville. She jumped at the chance, since it was only a couple of miles away and offered an income which could help them in those hard times.

The village of Nesterville was formed when an American company took note of the amount of standing timber in the surrounding area coupled with a sheltered bay. 1906 saw the construction of a sawmill, office, warehouse, machine shop and company houses. Logs were dumped into the bay, from which they were drawn up into the mill to be sawn into lumber. A tramway extended out into the lake to allow boats to load the lumber. Operations began in 1907.

The village had grown quickly to around 400 people with a company store, a Catholic Church and a school. For a short two-year period, a second teacher was hired, but finances would not support this so the school reverted back to a single classroom with a large enrollment.

Unfortunately, the boom did not last long. Timber ran out and the mill burned down in the 1920's. Mr. Hern came home to help on the farm until his death. Many of the families moved away, but in 1941, mom still had a fairly large number of students in Grades 1 to 8.

I have heard her tell the story of one or two of the big boys who decided to test the new teacher. These older boys were bigger than her but the rebellion was short lived as mom claims to have hauled one of these boys out of his desk and given him a stiff shaking. Try doing that in our modern society!

The question, of course, was what to do with Allen. At first, mom was able to hire girls to look after me at home but when that failed, I was taken to school and older girls looked after me.

By the time I was four or five, I was sitting in with the grade one class at school.

The Inspector of Public Schools for the district was a kindly man named Mr. Geiger who encouraged mom to continue teaching on a letter of permission for many years. (He also gained my lasting admiration by giving me my first quarter!)

In visiting the school, he gave the children tests in arithmetic and other subjects. Since I was there, he gave me the Grade One test as well, and when he saw that I was able to do the work, he told mom to enroll me as a pupil so I started first grade at 5 years of age.

Mom loved her teaching and loved her pupils. In later years, as an elderly lady, she was thrilled to meet some of those students again and was always delighted that they remembered her as a good but very strict teacher.

Among the responsibilities of teaching in one room schools of that day was the preparation of the annual Christmas Concert. These community events were quite the productions involving solos, duets, and other musical numbers. There were also plays to put on involving the learning of lines as well as recitations by children of various ages. But perhaps the part that stood out in mom's memory was the preparation of drills.

As mom describes them, they all consisted of much the same movements. Each involved marching in quick, lively steps in circles and crosses with a song carrying the theme of the drill.

Mom reports, "One was the 'Alice Blue Gown Drill' - about 8 pairs of girls marching. All were dressed in gowns made of blue crepe paper with about 3 or 4 tiers of frills and pretty little blue hats to match. (The mothers' help in making the costumes added to the community spirit of the annual event.) Tinsel always gave a shiny glitter as they marched. At the mid-point, they took a position and all sang the Alice Blue Gown song as they continued the march to the end and again a position was chosen and the curtain drawn or they marched off the platform or behind the curtain to small rooms where they took off the pretty gowns.

"Other drills included a scarf drill, a flag drill, comic drills portraying imitations of farmers or comic actors such as Charlie Chaplin. There was an upside-down drill behind a curtain where each couple had shoes on their hands. Only the upside-down shoes showed above the curtain to look as though they had turned upside down and were walking on air.

"Each concert included the Christmas story or something of a spiritual nature."

Mom drove the family car to school but on one cold day, the engine coolants froze, and overheated the motor. A replacement motor was not satisfactory so, in 1949 dad brought home a lovely dark blue 49 Ford. To a ten-year-old, that was a pretty snazzy car. That car was at the centre of a romance in the Hern household.

Saturday night was 'farmer's night out' when many of the farmers went to town. Shopping was done and often the men gathered in Ralph MacKay's shop to talk about the week's happenings. I don't remember how the ladies and children entertained themselves.

Saturday night was also the dance at the Odd Fellows' Hall. One night while we were sitting in the car waiting on Norman to come, mom saw him coming up the street with a young woman, Jean Boville, and her brother Jack. Mom had a premonition that there was the girl Norman was going to marry, and indeed that is how it turned out.

After six or seven years of teaching in Nesterville, mom taught junior grades in the public school in Thessalon for 3 years, followed by years of teaching in the one room at school at Livingstone Creek, which was farther away.

Because of starting Grade One early, I entered high school at 12 years of age. That was a terrible mistake. I was not at all prepared socially for the challenges of high school. As a result, those were difficult and unhappy years.

Farm work included shoeing the horses, and repairing equipment. Dad had a blacksmith's forge and some basic tools, a vice and a piece of railroad rail out in the garage. He never did have an anvil.

There dad heated, hammered and reshaped steel while repairing farm machinery. He even replaced piston rings or ground engine valves in this building. He created and built a counter weighted slide door that went overhead, out of the way.

When it came to shoeing horses, he did not like the idea of putting a horse in a rack, as many others did. Instead, if a horse was difficult to control, he would have Norm or Gordon hold the horse by the halter. He had a stick with a piece of cotton rope threaded through one end like a needle, and this loop of rope was slipped over the upper lip and twisted tight to divert the horse's attention while it was being worked on, and - surprisingly, it worked.

As we consider the many things of which Lew Hern was capable, it is easy to see that here was a gifted man who could turn his hand to almost anything successfully. I am not sure that we always gave him the credit he deserved.

Because of being the youngest, I was not expected to help on the farm to the same degree as my brothers, and spent more time around the house helping mom. Housekeeping was not one of mom's great loves, so when company was coming, I would be pressed into service to help with dusting and cleaning while 'stuff' got thrown quickly into the back bedroom. My wife still kids me that since I had to do the dishes at home, how come I still don't know how to organize them for orderly washing? Organization was never a skill of either my mother or myself.

Mom and I remained very close. While dad was quite a serious man, mom was actually a bit of a 'live wire'. As an example, she would wrestle with Gordon and with me until we got too big for her to win. We used to joke about the fun we had when dad was away from the house. "When the cat's away, the mice will play". With mom, we could have a lot of good amusement.

When it came to discipline, I don't remember my dad ever touching me. He didn't need to. One stern word was enough to bring me into line.

There was no such thing as going out to play with friends. Our neighbours across the highway, Grace and Elmer Campbell had three children. Raymond would have been Gordon's age or older. Inez was a little older and Colin a bit younger than myself, and occasionally we got together to play but very rarely. Life was serious and for the most part I entertained myself by talking to myself out loud and making up all kinds of outlandish stories in which I was the hero of the plot! It was embarrassing though when someone was near enough to hear.

So we grew up. Middle age came and went for mom and dad, filled with hard work trying to keep body and soul together, just as was the case with so many others.

Those Good ole Days

When I go back in my thinkin'
To those days I knew before,
When we had the horse and buggy
And the five and ten cent store,
You may call me square and corny
When I sing and shout and praise
But we all were much more happy
Back in those good ole days.

Ev'rybody seemed more friendly
And the truth was more in style;
All you did to seal a bargain
Was a handshake and a smile.
And if you should fail or stumble
From the load you had to bear,
Helpin' hands with love and kindness
In a hurry soon were there.

Church and Sunday were more sacred,
And the preachin' was for real;
Sin was sin, and God was Holy,
And the Bible had appeal.
It was read with more conviction,
Not in portion, but the whole,
And before you fed the body,
It was read to feed the soul.

Good ole days, they're gone forever,
Never to return, they say,
They and God are too old fashioned
For this modern world today.
But to me, I'll be quite honest
With their slow and backward ways,
God was feared and more respected
Back there in those good ole days.

Written in "Homespun Gospel, the Poetry of Walt Huntley," Published by G.R. Welch Company Limited, 960 Gateway, Burlington, Ontario, 1981

Chapter Eight

Busy years

"Opportunity is missed by most people because
it is dressed in overalls and looks like work."
Thomas A. Edison

 s Gordon says, "Coming out of the Great Depression, and the Second World War were hard times and it is to the credit of our parents' struggle that our generation were the beneficiaries of their love and care. The poverty of those years scalded them with a fear of indebtedness to the point of caution and alarm when we of the next generation bought a new piece of equipment or anything on credit."

But while buying on credit was not likely, that did not mean that our parents did not go into debt.

That brings us to the Rowan farm on which mom had grown up.

While we have heard that Grandpa Rowan was a good farmer, the Rowan farm had been suffering from lack of attention. Mother's younger brother Clarence was a big, pleasant fellow, but he was not a farmer, preferring always to work in the bush. My brother Gordon recounts that in the spring of 1937, Clarence was late leaving the logging camp in which he had been working. Others had left earlier while there was still good sleighing, but Clarence stayed on too long. By the time he headed his team toward home, it was raining and he was trying to drive the team and sleigh on bare gravel.

He phoned home and asked Grandpa Rowan to bring the wagon to Wharncliffe in order to load the sleigh. Grandpa drove his team and wagon the 15 or so miles each way through a cold spring rain and soon after he and Clarence got home he came down with severe pneumonia. Grandpa was 72 years of age. According to Gordon, he was never the same after that and since Clarence's heart was not in it, the farm languished. It appeared that it might have to be sold.

From that time on, Grandma and Grandpa came to live with mom and dad until he died in April, 1945 at age 80.

In those days, in smaller communities, when a person died, their bodies were taken to the funeral parlour to be embalmed and then were brought back in the coffin to the house. There the open casket was on display in the living room, where neighbours and friends came to pay their respects. Often the funeral was conducted from the home. That was in keeping with the day when death was seen as a normal part of life.

I was six years old in 1945 when Grandpa Rowan was buried from our farm home in April. Then in June, Grandma Hern died in the Sault and her body was brought down and buried from our home. Two caskets in our living room within 2 months. Then the 2nd World War ended in August. Three significant events within four months. I have no memory of the first, a dim memory of the second and some memory of the joy brought on by the third.

Back to our story.

You heard in the last chapter that romance was in the air.

After a sufficient courtship, on June 24, 1952, Norman and Jean were married. I was the skinny 13-year-old usher with a smirk on my face. Gordon, I believe was best man. Following their honeymoon, Norm took his new bride to the big square house on the Rogers farm.

Gordon tells of the day, three years previously, when Norm and dad and himself walked through the fields on the hard snow crust as they looked over that property. With mom and dad's help, Norm bought that farm in 1949, and started into the dairy business on his own. In '52 he had a home to which he could bring his new bride.

The old farm home needed a great deal of upgrading. It wasn't a palace to which Norman brought his bride, but they were very obviously in love, and so such things were overlooked.

Over time, they did upgrade that farm home – beautifully.

The big square dining room and living room had hardwood floors and Jean applied a coat of wax to bring up their lustre. But what would she use for a polisher? She laid a big coat on the floor, had her 13-year-old brother-in-law lie down on the coat and then pushed me, pulled me around on the floor by my feet to do the job.

That home became the nest into which seven children were welcomed. One by one, Isabel, Keith, Phyllis Anne, Jenat, Glen, Beth and Ken were added. Oh, it was a lively place! Mom and dad's house was also a lively place when the whole family came to visit grandma and grandpa as well. I hope my nieces and nephews will forgive me if I include a little ditty I used to say when the family left for home. "The tumult and the shouting die, Norman and the kids depart!"

By 1950, Clarence was logging up the Mississauga River while the Rowan farm continued to be neglected. In time the excellent Sherwood farm was up for sale, whether as a bank foreclosure or tax sale, I am not sure.

It was just a year after mom and dad had helped Norman buy the Rogers farm, and they did not have the money to buy the Rowan farm. You can understand the pain in mom's heart as she saw the possibility of that land on which she had grown up being purchased by a stranger. Situated on the Sherwood flats, alongside the Little Thessalon River where it drains into the Big Thessalon River, the farm is well drained sandy loam soil - a highly desirable property.

What could they do?

The answer came in a visit from the Farquhars who lived across the road from the Rowan house. As Gordon tells the story, Mr. Farquhar told dad and mom, "We'd like to see you people get that farm."

That was a real kindness. They would loan mom and dad the money and hold the mortgage. According to mom, her oldest brother Leonard also sent $1,000.00 to help them. The farm was purchased. How pleased mom must have been to see her beloved Rowan farm safe.

For years, Grandma Rowan used to spend the winters with us and the summers in the old farm house in Sherwood. She also spent time with Clarence who was now living in Batchewana, where he married Leisa Neyland of Batchewana Bay. Their children are Andrew, Clyde, Linda and Leonard. In 1958 Clarence took his family west to be near his oldest brother, and there he took ill and died at 56 years of age.

That must have been very hard on Grandma Rowan.

Grandma Rowan, a most wonderful lady

My brothers and I had nothing but the fondest memories of this dear quiet little lady. Through the years of mom's teaching, Grandma lived with us and helped to look after me.

She occupied the front bedroom, and after she did the dishes at noon she would go in, lie down and sleep for about 15 minutes, then be back up refreshed. (Her grandson did not inherit this gift.)

One day she had gotten up from her nap and come back out to the kitchen when a tremendous thunder storm broke and a bolt of lightening struck the house. It passed through her bedroom, struck a metal bed lamp with a pull chain on the head of her metal frame bed. The lightening actually cut one of those little balls of the chain in half. In going through the floor, it ripped a section of the linoleum to shreds, with the pieces sticking into the wall paper that was on the ceiling. It then went through the floor into the basement splintering one of the floor joists but without starting a fire. Had she been in her bed, without doubt she would have been killed. How the house was saved from fire is a mystery.

Having Grandma in our home through my growing up years was a great blessing to me. I think that she is probably responsible for the fact that seniors have always found a soft spot in my heart.

Grandma died in 1957 when I was 18. I wrote a poem about her a few years later that expresses something of my feelings for her.

To Grandma,

I knew her not in the bloom of youth;
Ne'er saw her in her early years.
The years of toil had left their mark
Upon her upright frame before I first
set eyes on her and she on me.
The body, once so proudly held erect had
taken on a stoop, her shoulders sagged,
Her brow was wrinkled and her skin, once clear
and smooth, had lost its youthful beauty.

Her friends had mostly gone, her husband, too;
All called before to dwell on high with our Creator.
Yet she lived on, surrounded by the noise and
hustle-bustle of our modern world.
And I, in my exuberance, thought surely there could be
No one so wonderful in all the earth as this dear lady,
Who had always time to tell me stories of a by-gone day.
How often have I seen her in the grand old
wicker rocker that she loved so well;
Her Bible on her knee and magnifying glass in hand
To see the precious words that dwelt among its pages,
Her countenance a picture of serenity and peace.
How often would I envy her her simple way of life!
And now she's gone; and surely there's a little
piece of me gone with her. Yet if there is,
'Tis measure small for that she left behind
within the hearts of those who knew her,
And who miss the shuffle of her feet upon the floor;
Content to do the simple tasks and ever
conscious of the thing that needed doing.
To us it was a mighty loss. Yet there are
many such across the country,
And if every home could have just such a
lady in its midst, and every child know
The joy and happiness to be derived from simple things,
There could not be a single one too many.
We honour her;
And thus commend her to our maker.
We know that there she shall find rest
And greater peace among the ones she cherished long ago.
(Allen Hern)

The headstone for Grandma and Grandpa Rowan says, "Until the day break and the shadows flee away." Song of Solomon 2:17"

Now let me tell you a little more about my dad.

Lew Hern: a favourite picture of my dad

Dad was not a well man throughout my growing up years. Whether it was "farmer's lung" caused by dust, or whether it was the result of smoking, dad suffered from emphysema throughout a good part of his life. Dad was not a cigarette man. He smoked a pipe - or perhaps as we joked, he smoked matches, because he was always having to relight that pipe.

At Christmas time one of his gifts was usually a box of cigars. Typically, he smoked a couple of inches of the cigar, stubbed it out and put it on a tray on the clock shelf in the kitchen. I have not forgotten the winter day when I stole his cigar off the shelf, took it out on the back porch and had just struck the match when the inside door opened. Match and cigar flew out of my hand into the snow. A few days later dad asked me if I had seen his cigar, and of course I was as innocent as a lamb, while out in the snow, the imprint was still clearly visible. He knew the answer to his question but he didn't press the issue. When asking the family to give me memories of their grandparents, Keith tells me that he also sampled one of Grandpa's cigars.

I think that dad was always a bit accident prone. When Norman was still a young boy, dad was sawing lumber with what we called a drag saw. In the process, his hand got caught and he severed the little finger on his left hand. As he was walking to the house, with his hand in a bloody rag, Norman saw him and ran around him trying to see what had happened. Then he ran on ahead, calling, "Daddy cut his finger off!"

On numerous occasions, when climbing on ladders, he fell and cracked or broke ribs. In those days, doctors bound up a person's chest with tape until healing took place, a painful experience.

From time to time, dad would go down to the basement in his stocking feet, to split some kindling for the fire. On more than one occasion he put the axe into his foot and came back upstairs bleeding.

With Norman's property being about five miles west of us, and the newly acquired Rowan farm about four miles east of us, and one set of equipment serving the three places, it required moving things back and forth though Norm soon got his own equipment.

Whatever the cause, Dad's health suffered.

His illness was finally diagnosed as stomach ulcers. Perhaps it was an allergy to milk as my brother has suggested. When I was still fairly young, he went into hospital where three quarters of his stomach was removed. Before the operation, dad is reported to have asked the doctor, "Hey, doc, I'd like you to do something for me." "What's that, Lew?" "When you remove that part of my stomach, I want you to put it into formaldehyde and save it for me." The old doctor is said to have turned toward the door, then turned back to say, "Hern, you didn't look after it when you had it, and you're not getting it back now!"

The same doctor was asked by dad at a later time to give him something to help him to put on some weight. He was about 5 foot nine inches and weighed about 127 pounds throughout the years that I knew him. The old doctor is said to have reached out and pinched dad's ribs saying, "Oh, Lew, you can't put meat on a greyhound!" That was certainly true, and he never did gain weight.

I remember the time when I caught a glimpse of dad's financial situation. At that time, when you took your cheque to the bank or went to withdraw money, you gave your pass book to the teller who recorded the transactions. As a youngster, I naturally felt that with the income from the milk cheques, dad must be doing alright. But one day I saw his pass book and it had a great deal of red ink which told of running a deficit. Gordon also records a day when dad complained to him, "Gordy, we just don't seem to be able to get ahead."

I always had the sense that dad felt that Bill Tremelling, his neighbour and friend, was much more well off than himself. I think that this was hard on my father.

One thing that I will not forget about dad was his blue serge suits. Every few years he would go to the Sault to H & R Lash's Men's Wear where Charlie Murphy would tailor his latest three-piece blue serge. Dad did not have a lot of money but when he bought something he valued quality, and that is what Lashes gave him.

He was a responsible and social person, with a strong interest in what was going on in the community and the country. Over the years he was at various times on the School Board, on the municipal council, and on the milk trucking committee. He was also a long-term member of the Masonic Lodge, as a member, a master and a past master of that organization. Both my brothers also became masons, for at least a time.

Gordon says that he was also instrumental in getting the attention of the Great Lakes Power Company to extend the power lines beyond Bruce Mines to near Thessalon, which had its own power at that time. It was this extension which brought electricity to our farm.

Like his father before him, dad was a keen Conservative member. The Conservative MPP in our area for many years was Johnny Fullerton who grew up on a farm just west of us. Johnny was also a local businessman and had the funeral parlour. His office was in the store, and dad loved to go in to visit with Johnny with whom he could talk about the ups and downs of the political scene and get the latest news about what was happening in the larger world.

At times he wrote things for the Conservatives, and travelled with our later member of parliament to some of the meetings.

As I have said, dad was a serious man. He had been through tough times and tended to predict more difficult times ahead.

I remember the day when a strange car drove into the yard and four men got out. Dad actually had to climb out from under his own car to speak to them, and I suspect that he had a sinking sensation as he met these strangers. Sure enough, one of them showed some form of identification from the taxation authority.

After the war, he had sensed that the government would start investigating farmers for income tax purposes. As a result, he began faithfully keeping bills and receipts in a box in a drawer, but not organized for ready reference. Now he had to submit that box to the scrutiny of this tax man.

For the next couple of days that fellow went through dad's records while the others went on to annoy other candidates. Subsequently, my parents were billed for sixteen hundred dollars in tax arrears which strained mom and dad's combined efforts to scrape up the money

We sometimes called him a pessimist, but he said, no, he was a realist. As Gordon says, "Dad's life, his thoughts and desires were not necessarily shared by his family, and I'm sure that he, at times, felt estranged and unappreciated."

Over all those years, our own firewood was brought out of the bush by horses and sleigh and thrown into a pile. A lot of these blocks were large maple and birch, and very difficult to split.

In his older frail state, dad did not hesitate to go out with his axe and work around each block, taking slabs off till he worked his way into the middle. For the extremely tough blocks, he used a steel wedge and the sledge hammer. Apparently at one point he was told that he should consider getting a power splitter, but I don't remember if he ever got one.

Meanwhile, mom was busy with school. In those early days, she used a hectograph – a thin layer of gelatin on a tray. A page of math problems or other seatwork was printed by hand on paper with a purple hectograph pencil. The paper was then laid face down on the gelatin base, transferring its image into that substance. Clean sheets of paper were then pressed onto the hectograph one at a time to get as many sheets as needed. (Would you believe that you can google this and buy these supplies on the internet even today?)

Mom was also active within the Ladies' Aid of the United Church.

Busy years. Tiring years, Better times were coming as dad and mom began to see the fruit of their labours.

Chapter Nine

The Fruit of their Labours

"There is no boon in nature.
All the blessings we enjoy are the fruits of
labor, toil, self-denial, and study."
~ William Graham Sumner

In 1950, dad sold the back farm to Bill Tremelling Junior. The sale meant that the cattle had to be brought to the place along the highway. It did not have an adequate barn in which to milk the cows or store the feed so a building program had to be engaged in.

From the bush on the back place, dad and Gordon had harvested two straight spruce trees. Using a broad axe, dad squared those two timbers to become the two main beams in the erection of the new barn. A new stable and milk house was installed so the dairy business could continue. That barn served the purpose for a few years until it was necessary to move the cattle to the farm at Sherwood. I don't remember the building of that barn. I believe that dad and Gordon accomplished that task. I did join in milking cows by hand during those years.

Now came one of the fruits of those hard years that probably came from the sale of the back place.

Mom and dad had friends who had a cottage on Basswood Lake. I was only six or seven years old when we visited with them and their daughter tried to teach me to swim. She didn't succeed nor has anyone else in the years since.

Basswood is a really lovely lake about 13 miles long by about 4 miles wide perhaps twenty miles or so north of Thessalon.

The idea of having a cottage on the lake appealed to dad, and he decided to buy a lot just up the beach from their friends, the Feagans. He brought a small building from the farm and added to it and there he had his cottage. It was very rustic, gradually being improved over time. It was his little hideaway.

Gordon was doing a lot of the farming so none of the family were free to spend much time at the lake. Dad went by himself, often just for the day, and there, after a life of hard work, he found a place of peace and tranquillity.

Unfortunately, Mom didn't share his enthusiasm. She says, "Due to my childhood fear of water, I had no desire to be near it nor in it. I never wanted to be away from my own room or home at night and I had no desire to go to the cottage."

As mom continues the story, "One day the Ladies' Aid was to meet at our house and we decided to take them to the cottage for the meeting and the day. I had the cottage all cleaned up and was all set for a good day. There were about 15 of us.

Lew and Gordon had gone to the Soo that day and at 3 or 3:30 p.m. they drove in with a lovely cedar strip boat with a ten-horsepower motor that Lew had bought. They unloaded it and our meeting was never finished. Everyone was so excited and Lew was in his glory. They got the boat into the water and everyone was crowding around, wanting a ride in it.

"The afternoon went on until everyone had a ride, all but me. I wasn't going to go out in that boat. Finally, Lew said, "Come on, I promise I won't go fast, and on that promise I went. It was a lovely ride and all went well for a while until Lew opened it up so fast, I was scared stiff. He broke his promise and I said, 'I'll never go in that boat with you again,' and I never did."

I feel sad that mom was unable to enjoy the cottage with dad. His brother, Uncle Herb later bought a cottage for Aunt Carrie, where they spent whole summers of enjoyable time together. I still mourn for the loss of the true companionship mom and dad could have shared there together.

Here at the lake, we once again see something of dad's versatility. The shore in front of the cottage was rocky, and not suitable for tying up the boat. This led to the building of a dock and a boathouse but how to get the boat into it was the next challenge.

Somewhere, he found some steel rails which he laid from the boathouse out over the rock and well out into the water. A carriage was then developed with steel wheels that could be backed down into the water to receive the boat. A winch cable fastened to both the carriage and the boat allowed both to be hand-cranked to lift the boat out of the water. Even though he was in ill health, he could handle the launching and putting away by himself.

Basswood had various species of fish, but lake trout were the ones for which dad fished. Friends showed him the right rod and reel with a leaded line which would sink, and the minnow harness with which the bait could be attached to the hook. There, all by himself, he would fish, with some success.

His neighbours, the Curries, were worried about him, warning us that in his weakened state, he could fall out of the boat and drown. Neither my brothers nor I had a desire to restrict his enjoyment of this pastime, and he never did have an accident right up to the time he sold his hideaway.

There was one other attraction along the very rugged road in to his property. The road ran through rocky hillsides on which blueberries were plentiful. There he picked pails of wild blueberries which we all enjoyed. Sometimes the family joined him in this endeavour.

All through these years, mom continued to teach school, still on a 'letter of permission' which had to be renewed on a regular basis.

Finally, she decided to do something about it.

Much to our surprise, she enrolled in the local high school in Bruce Mines when she was over sixty-five years of age. In that year, she passed the three subjects that she had never completed. She did well, and the kids in high school who were the age of her grandchildren accepted her as one of them. Now at last she was able to secure her permanent certificate which she used to complete her teaching years back in Nesterville, where a new school had replaced the old one.

In 1956, Gordon and dad reached an agreement by which Gordon could take over the farm, and, fresh from high school, I joined him in that effort as a kind of very junior partner.

With Gordon carrying the load of the farm, there was a desperate need to develop the Sherwood place, because the acreage at the home place was not adequate.

Once again, there was the need to expand the barn. To get ready to do so, the stable walls were removed just in time for a very strong wind to cause the barn to fall. I remember standing there, looking at that disaster, and wondering what was to be done.

Gordon picks up the story:

"Dad's lack of physical strength had let him out of the picture, but during the building of the new barn in 1958, he saw the need to replace an old carpenter whose abilities were unsatisfactory. Certainly, he had the knowledge and experience and the work was done."

Another farmer whose property had been divided by a highway upgrade, allowed them to secure half a barn which was of much the same dimensions as ours. It was taken down, brought home, and prepared for the new construction. But there was a problem.

When the collapse of the old barn took place, most of the beams had their tenons broken off, so Gordon says that a boring machine was borrowed, holes were bored into the ends of the beams and new tenons put into the ends of those timbers. By this means, they could be securely attached to the upright posts and raised, bent by bent to form the frame of the new structure.

Although Gordon says that I helped with the pouring of cement for the new foundation, I really have no memory of the erection of that new barn. The reason for that will show up in a few moments.

"Sixty-two years later that barn stands as a tribute to him," says my brother, "and in humility, I wish to express my appreciation for the contributions and sacrifices that parents make toward their offspring's development and success."

Probably the reason for my lack of memory was that that was the summer in which I almost died of peritonitis as I shall tell you as I write about a shift in direction.

The Hern Family 1953 Front tow: Mom, Grandma Rowan, Jean with Isabel. Back row: Allen, Dad, Gordon, Norman.

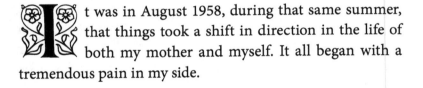

Chapter Ten

A Shift in Direction

"Sometimes the smallest step in the right direction
ends up being the biggest step of your life."
~ Emma Stone

It was in August 1958, during that same summer, that things took a shift in direction in the life of both my mother and myself. It all began with a tremendous pain in my side.

Pulled up short:

While I was at a dance in the Oddfellows' Hall in Thessalon, there came a sharp stabbing pain, which continued after I got home. It continued the next day, and the next. By the third day, mom began to get very worried and wanted to call the doctor.

I tried to stop her from doing so, and assured her that if dad brought home a laxative, I would be alright because a good bowel movement would cure the problem.

Mom called the doctor anyway. When she described my symptoms, he immediately said, "Under no circumstances let him take a laxative." So mom and dad took me to the Red Cross hospital in Thessalon.

The doctor checked me and kept me overnight. At some point the pain went away and the doctor planned to keep me for another night, but reluctantly agreed to make arrangements for my admission to the hospital in Sault Ste Marie.

In the Sault, Doctor West, and a surgeon, Dr. Baar, were waiting when we arrived quite late in the evening. By about 1:30 in the morning, I was on the operating table.

For about four days, I thought I was fine, trying to joke with the nurses and my room mate. I never was particularly conscious of being seriously ill. Nevertheless, I was kept in hospital for almost three weeks.

When mom and dad came to take me home, mom told me that I had been much more ill than I had realized. At the point at which the pain had stopped, my appendix had burst, and peritonitis had been at work in my system. Even after surgery the doctors had to fight to save my life. On the fifth night my aunt Alice was up through the night praying for me. The next morning the doctor agreed that her prayer was certainly of value at that point.

When mom and dad left the room after giving me that news, I was shocked.

Like most young people, I thought that death came to old people, not to nineteen-year olds.

You remember that in an earlier chapter I said that while I believed everything about God, I was very conscious of my sin and shortcomings. Still, I had always believed that if I was ever to face death, I would have an 'eleventh hour' to make things right with God. Now I faced the reality that I had come close to death, with no awareness of that fact.

I dropped my head back on the pillow and confessed to God that if He had let me die, I would have been separated from Him forever. I thanked Him for sparing my life and asked Him to allow me to serve Him in some way so that I might 'repay' Him for His mercy.

A new opportunity:

Although I am writing mom and dad's story, what follows sounds as though I have shifted the emphasis from them to myself. I include this because, as the cottage was the fruit of dad's labour, in many ways my life was part of the fruit of mom's life.

As I mentioned in the last chapter Gordon had taken over the farm from dad and I had been working with him for these three years. As I recuperated that fall, I had a visit from Mr. Geiger, our school inspector, whom you met in chapter seven (Busy Years). He came to ask me if I would like to teach school starting in January 1959. The teacher in the one room school at Dean Lake, Ontario was having to resign due to her pregnancy, and they needed someone to complete the year.

When I asked Gordon what I should do, he said that I should take the job, since I would never make a farmer anyway. Gordon does not remember having said this, but he was just stating the obvious.

My teaching years:

With no training other than my years of watching my mother, and some supply teaching in the Thessalon Public School, I took responsibility for 21 students in Grades 2 -8 in a country school that still had a wood stove which was kept fueled by Don Ingram, one of the Grade 8 boys.

When I took that school, I was absolutely sure that this was God's answer to my prayer on that hospital bed that I might have opportunity to serve the Lord. Though I prayed, I had not yet yielded my life to the Lord Jesus. Yet I was certain that it was God who had opened up this new direction. As I told my mother at the time, I did not really expect that teaching would be my life work. This was only a first step toward that to which I had felt called from childhood. I believe that she was pleased.

The months soon passed and my term at Dean Lake closed and with it, the closure of the school. As I wrote in my journal, "Although I made many mistakes, it was a start, and I thoroughly enjoyed this my first teaching experience."

During those few months of teaching I gained a new respect for my dad, and a new relationship with him. Normally, I drove his DeSoto car the 30 miles to and from the school. One morning I hit a patch of black ice, and watched as the car drifted toward, then settled into a hydro pole. I caught a ride home and told dad what had happened, and without a word of reproach, he simply said, "Take your mother's car. We'll look after this one." At that point I realized that dad had accepted me as an adult, and we became more like friends than father and son.

A new direction for mother and son.

From the time I was a baby, I had been faithfully taken to the United Church, where we had a succession of ministers: Rev. Beveridge, Rev. Dickinson, Rev. Pickell, Rev. McEachern, Rev. Gostonyi, Dr. Semple. They were all good, earnest men, preaching in a four-point charge: Zion United in Thessalon, Livingston Creek, Little Rapids, and Alma Heights - not an easy task for any man.

I have already described the family atmosphere of the 'little white church on the hill.'

These were our friends, and in a church sense, our family. When mom got her first fur coat, Bill Tremelling made her laugh with a certain amount of chagrin, as he teased her, "My, what they can do with rabbit skins these days!" Every one of those friends and neighbours I remember with fondness.

However, for some time mom had been concerned about the direction of the United Church. The minister began to use another version of the scriptures. Today we are quite used to other versions but at the time this seemed to be a rejection of the Word of God for the King James Bible was "the authorized version.". Then, the New Curriculum was brought out calling into question the first eleven chapters of Genesis, creation and other Biblical accounts. Having taught the Women's Bible Class for years, this change was troubling to her.

Thus it was, that the way had been prepared, when in 1957 Harold Wagler came to our door selling Watkins products. We learned that he and his wife and family had come to Thessalon to share in the leadership of the Brethren Assembly.

Mom and I began attending the Bible Chapel in the evenings, while still attending Alma Heights United in the afternoons.

For me, those evening services were a breath of fresh air. The first thing to attract my attention was the singing. What vibrancy there was in those songs!

> *"Praise the Saviour, ye who know Him,*
> *who can tell how much we owe Him?*
> *Gladly let us render to Him*
> *All we are and have."*

"To God be the glory, great things He hath done.
So loved He the world that He gave us His Son,
who yielded His life an atonement for sin,
and opened the life gate that all may God in."

"In my heart, there rings a melody,
there rings a melody with heaven's harmony.
In my heart there rings a melody,
There rings a melody of love."

This is just a sampling of the gospel messages contained in these lively songs These were far different from the hymns in the United Church Hymnal. I had never heard such joyous singing in my life. As Harold stood at the front leading them, the colour would climb up his face accenting his fervour. To this day, I love to sing these glorious songs of praise and witness of the grace of God to sinners such as I am.

The next thing that caught my attention was Harold's preaching. He did not have some highly educated treatise on some current theme. Instead he stood at the front of the church with his Bible in his hand, and preached verse by verse through a passage of scripture. Because we all carried our Bibles and followed along, I could see with my own eyes that he was giving us an explanation of exactly what was written there. As I listened from week to week, I acknowledged to myself that if the Bible is true, then he was giving me the truth for I could see it for myself.

Here there was no questioning the Word of God. It was preached without apology and with passion. Whatever was in the passage was exactly what was set forth, explained and illustrated. From week to week he preached his way through a book of the Bible, and so the whole word of God was being opened up to us.

How the Word of God convicted me! Every time he preached, from whatever passage, I was convicted of my sinfulness and of my need of a Saviour.

I loved that preaching, and I loved that man. I knew that he cared about me, and that God loved me with such an everlasting love that His Son Jesus came from heaven and went to the cross to pay for my sins and failures.

It did not take long for me to realize that if I were to respond to that preaching, my life would have to change. But there was an ongoing battle in my heart, because while one part of me wanted to yield, another part of me did not want to change. I have often said that during that period, I hated myself for my sin, but I loved my sin. And so the battle raged. I have always said that when I shook hands with Harold at the door and he beamed at me, asking how I was, I knew that I was lying though my teeth when I assured him that I was 'fine.'

While this was happening to me, mom was being deeply affected as well. She had been a sincere Christian woman throughout her adult life but she had not been well taught. As I have said, for years she had taught the women in the adult class in Alma Heights United. Without doubt, she had studied the Bible earnestly for those lessons.

Now, sitting under consistent teaching of the Word, she began to understand more fully what salvation was really all about. She says of herself, "I began to understand things I had never really been sure of before. Now I knew that I was a sinner saved by grace and my life began to change."

Again, I want to affirm, this did not make her perfect. Failure to live out fully what we know to be the truth is a universal failing of humans and it was no different with her. But there was a joy and a pleasure in hearing the Word faithfully taught which those who have known it will understand.

Mom Hern – Mom and I were very close ***

The real change for me came a couple of years later.

Four young men from Toronto Bible College came for a week of special meetings which were held in the Oddfellows' Hall. I was curious to hear these fellows. They were all from overseas, and all spoke with accents which I didn't care for.

One of them, Barry McGrath, was from New Zealand, and in testimony told of being a pop singer in his home country. He claimed that he loved singing in front of adoring fans, and determined to come to the United States to get to the top of his field. He told of coming to Canada, and of the way in which God drew him to Himself. Leaving the music field, he was at Bible School, training to be a Pastor or missionary. Listening to him, I was sure that he was boasting, and felt critical of every word he spoke.

But following his testimony, he sang a song in the most beautiful tenor voice I had ever heard, and I knew this was no empty boast. It was this song, which reached through to my heart.

Jesus, my Lord will love me forever,
From Him not power of evil can sever,
He gave His life to ransom my soul -
Now I belong to Him!
Now I belong to Jesus, Jesus belongs to me.
Not for the years of time alone, but for eternity.

Joy floods my soul, for Jesus has saved me,
Freed me from sin which long had enslaved me;
His precious blood, He gave to redeem -
Now I belong to Him.
Now I belong to Jesus, Jesus belongs to me.
Not for the years of time alone, but for eternity.

Not that night, but the next day, I acknowledged my need of a Saviour and invited Jesus to come into my life and take control. This is in keeping with many scriptures including **John 5:24 *"Most assuredly, I say to you, he who hears My word and believes in Him who sent Me has everlasting life, and shall not come into judgment, but has passed from death into life."***

In all the earlier years when I had wrestled with my need to accept the Lord Jesus, I had held back out of a fear of what that would cost me. Now at last I could hold back no longer.

In the days, months and years that followed I saw that there had been a real change. In sitting under the preaching of the Word of God which had previously **convicted me** in every service, the Word now **comforted** me as I accepted the fact that I had been forgiven and brought into the family of God. What a wonderful change.

Following the school year in Dean Lake, I enrolled for teacher's training in what was called 'the completing course'. In this you took a six-week summer course, taught for a year, took another summer course, taught for another year, followed by one year at North Bay Teacher's College. Two more years of teaching secured a permanent certificate. I believe that this method of teacher training was discontinued the next year.

During that first summer course which was held at the Western Technical and Commercial School in Toronto, I had the great good fortune of rooming with a man who became a life-long friend. Ken Raaflaub was from Magnetewan, Ontario. He too was a Christian, a member of the Lutheran Church (Missouri Synod). What a great friend he became.

One other significance of that summer was an overall change of outlook on my part.

I mentioned my lack of emotional preparation for high school. This was all part of a huge sense of insecurity. Because I was never sure that I was accepted by others, I had developed a habit of talking too loudly and trying to push myself into the conversation with others. Of course, the harder I tried, the more people resisted, and the more insecure I became.

That summer, I determined that whether I passed or failed the course, I was going to learn how to be a friend to the others in the class, and entered with that uppermost in mind. As I met people, I consciously set out to show an interest in them and to listen to them, rather than talking about myself. Three days later, I was chosen to represent our form on the Students' Council. That was a huge step for me, and the following summer, I was once again selected.

I believe that this new realization that the way to make friends was to care about them and to listen to them became an important building block in preparing me for later pastoral ministry.

Yes, a change of life, and a change of direction for both mom and myself. I can assure you though, that those changes didn't happen overnight.

There followed a year of teaching at Livingstone Creek School (once more following in mom's steps). While teaching, I continued helping on the farm with evening chores and on weekends. On Sunday evenings, Mom and I were always in the Thessalon Bible Chapel, rejoicing in God's goodness to us as we listened to Harold preach the Word. Of course, mom was thrilled by the change she saw in me, and we became even closer. Happy years.

In another summer school in Toronto, Ken and I once more roomed together, enjoying one another's company.

In the 1960 - 61 year, the local schools around Thessalon were amalgamated into a new four room Central Public School located at Little Rapids. I taught 43 pupils in Grades 5 and 6. In my journal I report "a most enjoyable year and very successful." Then off to North Bay Teachers College for my full year of training.

One of mom's joys was the growing number of grandchildren in Norm and Jean's family. Isabel was born in 1953; Keith in '54; Phyllis Anne in '56; Jenat in 1960; Glen in 1962; Beth in'64 and Ken in 1970. It always made for a lively time when they came to visit.

It was also a special time when our relatives from the Sault would come down to the farm for a visit.

When Uncle Herb and Aunt Carrie came, she always managed to have a tub in the trunk in which she would get a tubful of well rotted manure for her garden. She had a green thumb and loved her flower gardens.

When Uncle Lionel and Aunt Alice Keith came, sometimes bringing Aunt Sadie and Aunt Eva as well, it was a little different. Aunt Sadie and Aunt Eva loved to go walking out in the fresh farm air, murmuring, "My, isn't nature wonderful?"

Uncle Lionel, on the other hand, was very much a city man. He had been born, I believe, in Croatia, and spent his working life in the steel plant in the Sault. I don't think that he was ever very comfortable on the farm.

I remember the day when we had a cow in the barn unable to deliver her calf. She was lying down in her stall, and Gordon had gotten a rope on the calf's front legs and was right down on the floor trying to pull this calf out. I believe I had gone to the house to get some hot water, and Uncle Lionel wanted to know what we were doing. I tried to put him off, but after a few minutes, here he came walking down the walk, good shoes and all. I'm not sure if the stable had been cleaned yet, but it was pretty messy. I assure you this 'birth' was not a pretty sight, and after a few moments of looking on, he turned and walked slowly around to the other side of the barn where he was sick to his stomach. Then he quietly left the barn and went back to the house. I don't think that they stayed for supper!

This seems like a good time to tell the story of mom's 'raspberry vinegar'. I don't remember how it was made, but it was a concentrate of which one would mix about three tablespoonsful in a glass of cold water. It made a quite refreshing drink. Well now for a memory ... or perhaps it was a story I heard ... about this special drink.

It seems that one or more of these aunts were visiting and mom gave nice refreshing glasses of this special nectar before they got in the car to go the 50 miles to the Soo. They headed out for home, but part way there, they had to get the car to stop so they could stand beside the car and throw up mom's favourite tonic. Apparently as a car went by, they heard someone call out, "There's somebody that has had one too many!" (This about ladies who were complete teetotallers.)

Hmmn, two stories in a row about getting sick from a visit to the farm. Is there a pattern here? ... my, isn't nature wonderful!!!

Chapter Eleven

New families established

> "God gave us memories that we might
> have roses in December."
> ~J.M. Barrie, Courage

> "Pleasure is the flower that passes;
> remembrance, the lasting perfume."
> ~Jean de Boufflers

> "The man with a clear conscience
> probably has a poor memory."
> ~Author Unknown

It was the fall of 1961when I left the Thessalon area where I had been teaching for 2 ½ years in order to attend North Bay Teachers College for my completing year.

As we had done for two previous summers, my chum Ken Raaflaub and I planned to room together. Following up a lead, we arrived at the home of Albert Springer, where Albert was working in his garden. Next thing we knew, he was showing us a rose, and preaching a little sermon to us. I soon discovered that Albert was an occasional preacher in the North Bay Brethren Assembly and in the local prison.

Albert, of German background was married to Eileen, who must have come right from the heart of Ireland. What a combination! Albert was staid and sober (I might almost say humourless, though he laughed at his own jokes!), while you could hear Eileen's laughter ringing out over the whole neighbourhood.

They took us in and gave us the upstairs of the house plus periodic food from Eileen's kitchen which helped out our bachelor-type creations.

It's interesting that Albert was always giving us little sermons, and took me with him once to the Brethren Assembly, but although I had become a Christian in the Brethren Assembly in Thessalon, I never went with Albert again.

Instead, that year I attended the large St. Andrew's United Church.

I no sooner arrived at that large city church than I was drafted into the choir. How that came about I have no idea! Coming from a country church, I had never sung in a choir before.

About mid-October, another person who came from a small United Church in the country also began attending. She too was also immediately invited into the choir. (They must have been quite a welcoming congregation!)

I have never forgotten seeing that beautiful young woman dressed in a red jacket arriving in the choir loft. It didn't take long to learn that she was from a farm on Manitoulin Island.

Do you believe in the providence of God? Even if you don't, and believe in fate or luck or karma, the results would still be the same. My favourite colour is red, and a girl from the farm is likely to be a good cook!! Now does it not seem obvious that a young woman like that, fresh from the country would need a fellow to walk her home after choir practice? I thought you would see it my way!

A strange twist to this story is that, like me, Sheila had been given the opportunity to teach school before she had any formal training. You remember Mr. Geiger, the school Inspector who encouraged mom to start me in Grade One at five years of age? You remember that it was Mr. Geiger who asked me to take over the Dean Lake School at nineteen years of age? He was also the school inspector for Manitoulin Island, where Sheila Simpson was a pupil at Tekhummah. She, too, had been accelerated in her schooling and had also graduated from Grade 12 at 16 years of age. There was a need of a teacher in Waldhof, near Dryden, Ontario, and Mr. Geiger enlisted this still 16-year-old to leave her home and travel by train to that community several hundred miles away to teach in their one room school. There she stayed with a German speaking family and had some exposure to a Baptist Church.

Looking back, it is hard to believe that this could happen. Neither of us had a teaching certificate, but there was a need, and Mr. Geiger had followed the progress of each of us through school. Strangely, he believed that each of us was capable of doing the job. Now we met and compared notes on the strange way in which our lives had paralleled one another even though we were from two different areas. How could it be that the two of us should meet in the choir loft of a church in a strange city? Unbelievable, but the rest, as they say, is history.

When each of us joined the choir, Mr. Victor Kviesis, a brilliant organist and choir director was leading the choir in the practise of the Christmas portion of Handel's Messiah. To a fellow that had not sung serious music before, that was a challenge! That is where I learned to sing tenor. I was fortunate to stand beside a well-trained tenor who also knew the music and knew how to read the score. I learned to sing the part by watching the notes with all their trills, hearing the music come into my ear and out through my mouth. Sheila was doing the same thing in the soprano section.

Mr. Kviesis seemed to have taken a liking to these two amateurs (though Sheila had been singing in choirs for years). Soon he chose us to sing in a quartette which was so challenging that it just about had Sheila in tears, but we did it, and have been singing together ever since.

I spoke about walking Sheila home after practice? I remember that it was snowing the night that I kissed her on the forehead. She did not object, and after that magical moment, I almost floated home in the freezing North Bay winter's night. It's strange but the several miles' distance never seemed that great as I walked those snowy miles to or from seeing Sheila.

Sheila was clerking in a ski shop that year, so we spent much time together.

I completed my course, enjoying my time with Ken and with Albert and Eileen Springer but you already know what was the real story of the year!

Neither of us has ever forgotten our first visits to one another's homes.

Sheila had told me that if her quiet English dad didn't like me, he'd just go off into another room and read. I must have been acceptable because he stayed in the room and her mom seemed to recognize that the visit had significance as well. Seems that there may have been a flush on Sheila's cheeks.

When we visited my home, we were in time to join the church family at a picnic, and Sheila was quite amused as my dad didn't know how to introduce her, so he called her "Allen's lady friend."

From that moment, dad and Sheila hit it off. How she loved her times with dad at the cottage when she had the chance.

With mom it took longer. You remember my speaking of how close mom and I were through all our earlier years. How was the young woman who was the love of my life to fit into this picture? Of course, I made a conscious choice in favour of Sheila, and mom no doubt felt a diminishing of our closeness. So, you see, this story is still about dad and mom as each of them adjusted to a new relationship.

The following year, it was Sheila who was in Teachers College, while I took up teaching in the Echo Bay Public School, about 20 miles east of Sault St. Marie.

Long trips from Echo Bay to North Bay took place about once a month interspersed with Sheila's visits to Algoma.

After completing her year in Teachers College, Sheila and her girlfriend Marj Baker took teaching positions in Tarentorus, one of the townships of Sault Ste Marie. Oh, joy, to have her in the same city, instead of several hours drive away.

1963. The time had come for mom to retire from teaching. Looking back on those twenty-two or twenty-three years since she had returned to teaching, mom wrote, "These last years have been a wonderful experience, and have only been accomplished by the help of a considerate husband and family, several splendid girls and women who have shared the household duties, and a loving mother who for fourteen years supervised the household and kept things at home on an even keel. It has been a pleasure to me to have had the privilege of sharing in the education of so many fine young people."

After another year of courtship, Sheila and I were married Aug. 12, 1964, in South Bay Mouth, on Manitoulin Island in the little United Church called 'St. Andrews by the Sea.'

I am not sure how mom felt about our marriage, but I do know that the inevitable took place. Although I still loved my mother, she had been replaced in my deepest affections and we were never able to be quite so close again. There was pain for both of us in that realization.

Two years later in 1966 it was Gordon's turn as he and Marjorie Mills were married. Marge's boys, Donald and Bruce joined them on the Sherwood farm. I believe that Gordon's marriage to Marge was the best thing that could have happened to him, because now farming had a purpose, and Marge, besides being a wonderful home maker, was a true helper and encourager.

At last Mom's boys all had partners and I believe Mom took real pleasure in each of us.

In preparation for writing mom's story in 2010, I asked the family to give me their memories of mom and dad. Isabel and Keith are the ones who knew her in her earlier years and they are the ones who shared their memories.

Isabel responded, "I have to try and think hard about my life with grandma but it sure was a good, fun loving time with her."

Isabel would have been 10 about the time mom retired, so her memories of a good fun loving time with her relates to a part of mom's life that my wife, Sheila, and our children never had a chance to know since she was almost 70 years of age when we were married. We never again lived close to Thessalon so my family had a limited opportunity to know her in her more fun-loving years.

Isabel continues, "My earliest recollection of grandma was starting at about the age of three, when I would go down to the farm and spend a few days visiting. The first thing that comes to mind is being there with great grandma Rowan, and of course I really thought that I was helping to look after her, as I recall she was almost bed ridden when I came along. I remember grandma having me go to the front bedroom to spend time with my great grandma, and one of my jobs was to comb her long hair and I was so proud to be able to help out. I remember great grandma quite well, as I spent many of my younger days with grandma and grandpa.

"When I was quite young, grandma took me to Thessalon and bought me a black doll. I still remember that doll to this day and would give anything to have that doll back. I don't know whatever became of it. It always stayed at grandma's and was mine to play with when I would be there.

"She bought me a black miniature china cup and saucer to have tea with her and when she was getting rid of things, to move to Algoma Manor, that tea set went to Stacey, her first great granddaughter.

"Before I was school age, grandma would take me to school with her for a day or so at a time. The schools that I attended were the Livingstone Creek school and Nesterville. I still remember a lot of the names and faces today.

"I remember spending weekends with grandma and going to church at both Alma Heights United and Thessalon Bible Chapel with her. She was proud to be able to dress me up in my Sunday best and show me off, and I was just as equally proud to be able to go with her. She often talked to me about

Christian faith, and I knew that grandma wanted her family to follow her in that direction. She was always disappointed that grandpa and the rest of our family stayed with the Alma Heights congregation and didn't transfer to Thessalon Bible chapel when the Alma Heights church had to be closed.

"Grandma liked to sew on occasion and a few times she made dresses or suits for me. Grandma had a dress form that we called Judy, and I recall putting clothes on Judy. I guess that was play time for me. Maybe that's why I still like to dress up today, as it was grandma's priority to be properly outfitted for every occasion. And of course, my doll took on the name Judy, I guess, from the dress form.

"One of my fondest memories of grandma were her preserves of pears and peaches. If Keith or I were at home sick, grandma always showed up with a quart of home-canned pears. It was like medicine to us and of course we took it and wanted more. I guess that's why I still like preserved pears today.

"Grandma wasn't one for spending a lot of time in the kitchen, but one of her great specialties was her famous sauerkraut. Even my mother couldn't perfect it as good as grandma."

I believe the sauerkraut came from both mom and Grandma Rowan, the cabbage chopped and put into the large crock with a plate weighted with a stone to add pressure. At least that is how I remember it. Funny I wouldn't have remembered the sauerkraut if Isabel had not mentioned it but I do remember that it was good.

Isabel continues, "As I became a teenager, I still remember going to spend time with grandma and travelling places with her in her Volkswagen beetle. She quite often would come up to our place and pick me up just to go shopping with her. I remember on many occasions going to the Sault and putting my info into clothes that she would be trying on at Tom Allen's Ladies Wear.

Keith writes, "I still catch myself thinking about some of the times we had as kids with our grandparents. I can not remember too many dealings with gramma other than being at Nesterville school and the picnics there, and Aunt Mabel coming to her house and making those cookies filled with raspberry jam." (Aunt Mabel was Mabel McCrea, Jean's aunt, and Keith's great aunt, who came once a week to bake and clean for mom. It's funny that Isabel mentions mom's lemon cookies. My memory is that it was Mrs. McCrea who made those lemon cookies which I can still taste in my mind, but raspberry? Oh, yes, now I remember - oatmeal cookies put together with raspberry jam! Thanks, Keith.)

Keith continues, "I remember more of grampa and our trips to the root cellar for potatoes and what seemed to be black carrots." (Carrots probably still covered with garden dirt, and the sand they were stored in.)

"I remember our days spent at Basswood lake and of course driving to Thessalon to get the daily news from Merv Wyman's shoe shop. Some things never change - now we just do it at the coffee shop each morning."

During those years mom and dad made more than one trip to Alberta to visit Mom's brother Leonard and Elva Rowan in Sylvan Lake with their children: Arthur and his wife; Enid and Jim Sharpe and their family; Phyllis and Neville Cannon and their boys; and Isabel and Danny Moore and their children.

Then on to Saskatchewan where they visited her other brother Garnet and Aggie Rowan in Tuxford, and their sons

Wally and Ted and their families. They enjoyed those times greatly, and it seems that our cousins enjoyed them too.

Cousin Isabel writes from Red Deere, "We all have great memories of your mother. Our children weren't very old when they last saw her, but Enid's older ones remember. We always had lots of fun with her.

"I must confess that I envied her for years. Mom and Dad used to tell us of her escapades, which I thought were very daring - but - it was the auburn hair that I really coveted. Mine was brown and I had all the freckles, so I couldn't see why I couldn't have auburn hair!

"When Enid and I took Dad to Ontario that last time, we stayed with your parents. Your mom drove us around and she and Dad would relive old times, with your mom pointing out different places while she drove. Enid and I sat in the back seat - slightly agitated - but the car seemed to know the road!!"

Ah, yes, memory. **"Pleasure is the flower that passes; remembrance, the lasting perfume."** That's true, isn't it, and in these later years of our own lives we treasure the fragrance of the past.

Meanwhile, in '64 – '65, mom was getting used to being at home rather than teaching, and dad was still enjoying his cottage.

After our marriage, Sheila and I attended First Baptist Church in the Soo, where Sheila was baptized as a believer in Jesus, and we joined as members. Of course, we sang in the choir and greatly enjoyed the preaching of Pastor Duncan MacGregor and the fellowship of Les and Isabel Tulloch and so many others.

During that year Sheila and I talked about my longstanding feeling of a call to the ministry, and she agreed to support me through school. That must have come as a surprise to both mom and dad and the rest of our family. Sheila's parents also must have wondered at this news. Their daughter had married a teacher not a preacher.

At Pastor Macgregor's suggestion I enrolled in the fall of 1965 in the four-year Bachelor's degree program at Central Baptist Seminary in Toronto, while Sheila took a teaching position in North York.

That next year, I was asked by Dr. Don Loveday who taught Pastoral Theology at the seminary to be his student pastor in Central Baptist Church in Brantford, Ontario. That was a wonderful experience and I was so glad that Sheila had the opportunity to get to know both his wife Nan Loveday, and his mother who had also been a Pastor's wife. I have been constantly thankful for the encouragement those two ladies were to Sheila during those eight months.

From that time on, we were out of the home area, so we can hardly record memories of the lives of mom and dad. How thankful we are for our sisters-in-law, Jean and Marge for the loving way in which they related to my mother. They provided the support which we were unable to do and we owe them a huge debt of gratitude.

When Sheila and I moved to Toronto to attend Seminary, dad and mom made a number of trips in her little Volkswagen, first to Toronto, and then to Port Perry where we had our first pastoral ministry.

Mom was over 70 years of age, and Thessalon traffic doesn't quite match that of Highway 400, so we were always a little nervous when we knew they were coming. Usually we went out to meet them at a junction on Highway 400, but on at least one occasion she surprised us by driving all the way into Toronto through that heavy traffic. After each visit we would take them out part way and then wave them off as they drove bravely toward home. We were always relieved when we heard that they were safely home.

By my third year in Seminary, Sheila and I began to desire to start our family, and by the grace of God, I was called to be the Pastor of Port Perry Baptist Church, north east of Toronto. I began ministry in February of 1968.

Juanita was born in April of 1968 and Sheila and the baby joined me in half of an old duplex in Port Perry. Though the church had had a succession of student Pastors who had come out from the Seminary on the weekends, we determined that we wanted to be the full time Pastor of the church. I therefore extended my Seminary studies for a fifth year while going into Toronto to the Seminary two days a week.

What a wonderful congregation for a young man who had not even completed his training. I have always said that if it had been left up to us to find the best church in Canada in which to begin ministry, we could not have chosen one better than Port Perry Baptist.

I have always marvelled that a young woman with as little background as Sheila had, became such an ideal Pastor's wife. (You'll forgive me for being biased.)

And so, mom's secretly held dream of a Pastor in the family came to fruition. Over and over again, in her letters and notes written in the late years of her life, Mom expressed her thanks to God for His goodness to her in blessing her with Norman and Jean and Gordon and Marge, and Sheila and myself. These were years of fulfillment for the long years of raising her family.

Dad and mom visited us in Port Perry on at least one occasion. When they came to Port Perry it was probably the first time Dad heard me preach. Having a personal interest in oratory, I'm not sure what dad thought of my sermon, but I have never forgotten his word of advice. "Preach practically." he said, "Preach practically."

Being a down to earth farmer, he was urging me to preach in a way that reaches people where they are, rather than with some theoretical explanation of scripture which might go over people's heads. That was good advice, since in many ways that's how Jesus preached, using parables about things with which the people were fully familiar. For fifty years I have tried to make sure that my preaching applies the scripture to peoples' real needs.

As I said, much earlier, I am surprised that dad said nothing to us about having been born in Port Perry or about the possibility that there might be relatives in the area.

In the next chapter, we'll say goodbye to dad, and watch mom adjust to a new life in her house in Thessalon.

Chapter Twelve

Major Change

"Change is the law of life and those who look only to
the past or present are certain to miss the future."
John F. Kennedy

t was about the time that mom retired from
a lifetime of teaching school that she became
interested in tracing her family history.

Fortunately, through all of this, we have a good record of
the remaining thirty-plus years of her life.

I nowadays find myself encouraging our Seniors to write
out their stories or record them on tape so that these histories
are not lost, for without recording them, the background of
their families is lost forever.

Memories of Dad.

In this chapter, however, I want to share a bit more about my
dad. In his retirement years he continued to enjoy a number
of interests.

He was interested in writing, and bought himself a typewriter on which he often wrote his thoughts on a number of matters.

I mentioned earlier that dad had always taken a strong interest in politics, and particularly in the Conservative party. For a few years he set out to help our local member of parliament, and wrote a number of pieces, even doing some travelling with him. If dad had had a more complete education, I believe he would have been very good at writing, but as it was, his spelling and grammar needed a good deal of help. I did some editing for him which I found very interesting and perhaps mom or others in the family did so as well. I found his writings to be well thought out, and very interesting, but he probably saw no need to keep them.

I have only one, which is on the subject of religion and which I value most highly. Let me share it with you. In it, he said:

"I cannot agree with the theory of modern technology, as they attempt to disprove certain historical Bible events that have a direct influence on man's relationship with God - disbelief in the chronicle of Noah's ark, the story of Jonah being swallowed by the whale, and the division of the Red Sea...

As a climax to all erroneous concepts, they hint of man's ability to question the power of God, even to the extent of casting doubts on the virgin birth of Christ. Always basing their theory on the assumption that such happenings were scientifically impossible. When the world is willing to admit that the power of God is Omnipotent, then they must also admit that God is the Master of all science."

I am so thankful that I have this one example of dad's very thoughtful response to those who would deny or dilute the Word of God.

Like all of us, dad had another side which sometimes showed up. My brother Norm writes, "Dad was not an easy man to live with - he ruled supreme. He would fly off the handle, and had a lack of compatibility."

Yes, he had a temper, that is true, which could flash unexpectedly, but not normally without reason. I'm not sure that we his offspring have entirely escaped that inherited temperament!

But as I have indicated, I was glad to have a good relationship with this man whom I came to respect with warm affection.

A humorous incident comes to mind.

When I was still a young adult, the United Church preacher wanted to have a layman's Sunday, and when he was lining up various men to take part, dad agreed to bring the message. I think he was looking forward to it, but when it came time to carry out his assignment, his nerves got the better of him. When I got home from morning chores, dad called me into the bedroom where he was sick in bed. He announced that he couldn't go to church and preach that sermon. He told me I was going to have to do it!

I knew it was his nerves that were bothering him and I said, "You're no more sick than I am. You got yourself into this and you can get yourself out of it."

I walked out of the room, and in a few minutes, dad was at the kitchen sink, shaving and he went to church and carried it off quite well, though I have no memory of what he said. I am still surprised at my boldness, and perhaps even more surprised that I got away with it.

In December of 1969, mom came to Port Perry to be with us while we waited for Ian to put in an appearance. That was a memorable visit, as on Christmas Eve day, my neighbour asked to borrow our 1965 Chevrolet car to go the 25 or so miles into Oshawa to pick up his cheque. Avery had a drinking problem, and I had tried for a year and a half to draw him back to the faith he had professed as a young man in Nova Scotia. Even when drinking, he revealed something of his background as we would sit together while he played his guitar and we sang "The Old Rugged Cross" and other hymns of faith.

Before loaning him our car that morning, he promised me that he would not drink. When the car was not back at 6:00 o-clock that evening, we were not surprised to hear the doorbell ring and to find a police officer with Avery in tow standing on our porch. "I'm afraid your car will not be coming home tonight," the policeman said, "It's wrapped around a cement bridge abutment down near Oshawa."

Avery himself was alright, so I told him to go home and enjoy Christmas Day and we'd talk after Christmas.

To this day we rejoice in the fruit of that experience because after Christmas, Avery genuinely renewed his commitment to the Lord Jesus, and he and Gloria together gave their lives over to the Lord's control. It was not long before Avery was playing his guitar and singing joyously in church those songs of faith. To this point over forty years later, Avery and Gloria have demonstrated the reality of the change that began that day. What is the loss of a car compared to a changed life?

We had one other guest in our home over that Christmas. Dale King, one of the students from Central Baptist Seminary was also with us and had a car, so I asked him if I could borrow it to take Sheila to the hospital when it was time. That time came in the early morning hours of Dec. 27. Dale heard us moving around and came out all nervous and concerned, wanting to know what he could do to help. We sent him back to bed but when I got home in the morning, having welcomed a new son into the family, Dale was just about in a panic. "Is Sheila alright? Is the baby O.K.?"

He could hardly believe that Sheila could have a baby without some terrible thing happening. Meanwhile, Sheila was fine. She is one of those ladies who, when she says, "It's time" you had to take it seriously because she didn't waste a lot of time in delivery.

Unfortunately, those were the days when the dads didn't get to stay with the mom through that awesome birth process. By the time Darryl was born in 1973, the doctor had agreed that I could stay with Sheila, but he was away when the time came and a country doctor took his place who wasn't comfortable with the practice so I missed out again.

In 1970 I completed my courses at Central Baptist Seminary and received my Bachelor of Theology degree. After 2 ½ years of pastoring a church while attending Seminary in Toronto two days a week, I looked forward to having my full time to devote to Port Perry Baptist.

But it was not to be. A letter came from Lively Baptist Church inviting us to candidate for the leadership of that congregation. At first, we said no, until the Lord made it clear that this was His will so at the end of December, 1970, our moving truck pulled up in front of the parsonage in Lively. What a reception we received! Over two feet of snow had been shovelled, and people were on hand to move our furnishings into the house. Quickly the ladies set up cribs and beds and soon 2 ½ year old Juanita and 1-year old Ian were settled in their beds.

What a surprise to find that our cupboards were stocked with food, and the fridge was outfitted as well.

Pastor of Lively Baptist Church - 1971 - 76

It was good to be much closer to both of our families. Within a little more than 2 hours we could be to Sheila's parents on Manitoulin Island or to Thessalon.

I wish we could have had more time with dad. From first meeting him, Sheila felt a strong attachment with him. I think she understood him as not everyone did, and I certainly felt that dad thought a great deal of her. How much more time she would have spent with him at the cottage if she had had the chance! But it was not to be.

In these later years, dad's health had been quite up and down, requiring recurring times in hospital. I used to say when he was recovering from one of his bouts, "Dad must be getting better, he's getting cranky!" I don't think this is unusual for those who are recovering and anxious to get on with life.

After enjoying the cottage for quite a few years, encouraged by the friendship of Jamie McCallum with whom he was able to share good chinwags, dad arrived at the point at which he sold his hide-away.

In a letter he had written to us after Ian was born, he spoke about the sale of the cottage.

"We have not had a bad winter so far, but some of the lowest temperatures that I remember for a good many years. There were two or three nights some thermometers in the district hit the low of minus forty. I will be glad to see summer coming again. Although in some respects I will miss those trips to the lake, I am really glad to have got rid of it. None of the rest of the family seemed to have any interest. I think they were only there once last summer and after Jamie McCallum died, none of my other neighbours seemed to fill his place and at times I found it a very lonesome place.

"When the weather gets to the place that we can depend on it, I am liable to drop in there without any announcement. I am very much interested in having a look at this new boy."

As we spent our first year in Lively, dad's health continued to go downhill and he spent more time in hospital.

I find it very interesting to look back to dad in his later years. As I write this, I am approaching eighty-one years of age, just a year younger than dad at his death.

Unlike dad, I have not had major health problems. Yes, I have experienced "atrial flutter" for which I was 'zapped' by the paddles to shock my heart back into rhythm. Because that did not last, I went to Vancouver for 'ablation' treatment which required a wire to be run up into my heart, so a particular spot could be burned to disrupt faulty electrical signals causing the arrhythmia. And yes, rheumatoid arthritis has brought about minor changes, but really, I am so much better than my dad at this age. I thank the Lord for this good fortune.

During his last hospitalization, an event took place which took us by surprise. Mrs. Lucy McDougall, a strong-minded Brethren woman, noted for being quite bold in her approach, visited dad and came away with an interesting story. Lucy was probably the last person I would have expected to have been accepted by my father.

According to her, she asked him, "Mr. Hern, before you married Mabel, did you love her?" I can almost hear my dad snort. He was not a man to suffer fools gladly. That was the kind of personal question dad would not think she had the right to ask, but apparently, he said yes. "Was she your wife, yet?" "No."

"Mr. Hern, she did not become your wife until you said, Yes, I take this woman as my wife and put the ring on her finger. Is that right?" "Yes."

"Mr. Hern, have you ever said 'Yes' to Jesus?"

According to Mrs. McDougall he answered, "No, I'm not sure I ever have."

"Would you like to?"

Again, according to her, he said yes, he would. And she claimed to have led him to ask Jesus into his life, to become his saviour.

Frankly, when I heard this story, I was highly sceptical. This did not ring true with the father with whom I was familiar. Did she take advantage of some weakness on his part? Did he fully understand what she was asking him?

If you share my scepticism at this point, don't stop reading yet.

If you have read chapter seven of this story, you will remember that I drew out the picture that, like myself, I was sure that dad believed every truth about God and the Lord Jesus. I am sure he did not doubt His sacrificial death to pay for all that separates us from God, His resurrection and ascension back into heaven. I asked at that point, "Is just believing the teaching of the Bible enough?" People will answer that question in different ways.

But wait, this is not the end of the story.

On a Monday evening at end of October, 1971, I received a phone call from mom saying that dad was asking for me. I drove the 2-hour drive home, arriving well on toward midnight.

Dad was waiting for me, and related to me a type of vision in which he seemed to be a detached spectator watching the same scene in 3 parts. The first involved a family at odds with each other, but suddenly the power of Christ transformed the family. Next was an industrial setting in which management and workers were deadlocked in strife, but in a moment the power of Christ transformed the situation giving peace to workers and management. The third scene was of two armies ready for battle when the power of Christ transformed the opponents and brought peace instead of bloodshed.

He wanted to know what I made of this strange experience and I confess that I did not have any easy answer for him, except to assert the message of scripture that the Lord Jesus will ultimately win the victory over all opposition. This seemed to satisfy him and he said, "Go to bed now and we'll talk again in the morning."

The next morning, while perfectly rational, dad referred again to what he had told me, and acknowledged that he had called for me, "because it would be easy to be taken for a fool in this matter." By this he demonstrated quite conclusively that this "vision" had caught him by surprise as much as its telling may surprise my readers.

He then said something I did not expect to hear.

"You know that little Mrs. McDougall? She visited me in the hospital and in about 20 minutes she preached the best message to me that I have ever heard from any preacher."

I knew then that this was not just a claim of Lucy McDougall, but it was evidence of a movement of God in dad's heart. Yes, dad believed throughout his life, but somehow Lucy had made it personal, and helped him to realize a more personal relationship with the Lord Jesus than he was used to. Whatever people may think, that is a valuable matter to consider.

That day dad impressed upon me and repeated this simple message, **"Al, preach the power of Christ is over all!"**

He then gave me his wishes for his funeral.

When I left his room that morning I said to mom. "It won't be long, now." He died two days later.

His obituary reads in part, "Lewis N. Hern... passed away November 3 at the age of 82. Mr. Hern always took an active interest in community, municipal and political affairs; as well as being an elder in the former Alma Heights United Church. He was a valued member of the Masonic Order.

"His funeral was from Zion United Church, Thessalon and was largely attended. Rev. Clyde Taylor conducted the service, assisted by Mr. Phillip Norbo of the Thessalon Bible Chapel. Mrs. Muriel McPhee as soloist sang 'Face to face with Christ my Saviour', an old favourite of the deceased."

A new life in Thessalon

I entitled this chapter," **Major Change**", and so it was.

Shortly after dad's funeral, mom sold the farm and rented a small home in Thessalon from Doug Rankin.

She writes, "I moved into my rented home Dec. 6/71, and from then on life changed and so did I. She was 76 years old, with 19 more years before the Lord took her home.

Before I conclude this chapter, let me share a few more memories from ones who remember her with fondness.

Granddaughter Isabel writes, "As I became a teenager, I still remember going to spend time with grandma and travelling places with her in her Volkswagen beetle.

"When Ron gave me my engagement ring in 1971, of course we had to go and show off this excitement to grandma and grandpa. That was an exciting time for both of them to see their oldest and first grandchild soon to be married the following summer. Grandpa passed away three weeks later and that was always a disappointment to me that he never got to attend the wedding.

"When Derek was born in 1973, grandma was again excited and very happy to have the great grandmother title. When both of our children were born, she made baby quilts for the children that have been passed on to Derek's children."

Inez Campbell who grew up on the farm across the highway writes, "At this time I must say, your Mother was one of my Mom's best friends. When Mom was so housebound, your mother would keep her in mind, and come and see her, and if Mom was able, take her places." (Grace Campbell suffered from crippling arthritis which put her at last into a wheelchair.)

Inez continues, "It however got too much for your Mom to help her up as she could not stand up on her own. Your mother still came to see her. When Mom went to the Manor (for eight months) after Dad died, your Aunt Sadie was in the next room and your mom came to see them both which made it nice for them."

Such was the joy of mom's heart after she moved to Thessalon. For several years, she enjoyed a greater usefulness than ever before, but that is the subject for another chapter.

Chapter Thirteen

Mom's Best Years

"Youth fades; love droops; the leaves of friendship fall;
A mother's secret hope outlives them all."
—Oliver Wendell Holmes

s mentioned at the close of chapter twelve, mom's move into Thessalon after dad's death opened the door to what I believe were probably the best ten years of her life. In those years from 1971 - 1981, or from 76 years to 86 years, she enjoyed a greater freedom to pursue new interests and a greater usefulness than ever. Let me tell you about it.

A new home

In a most interesting letter written to mom July 23, 1972 her Alma Heights friends expressed their best wishes.

"Dear Mrs. Hern,
We, your neighbours and friends, old and new, have
gathered in the traditional Alma Heights manner to honour

you on your retirement and departure from your former home in the community.

As a bride you came to our small hamlet and with your customary energy, abounding enthusiasm and talent along with your unlimited capacity for work, you soon became a real part of it, both in religious, educational and in our rural entertainment.

We all deeply regret that this occasion could not be shared by your husband, but we have a distinct feeling that he is spiritually present and from the Great Beyond is bestowing his blessing.

In your new home which is already blossoming with flowers of your own planting, we wish you the joy and happiness which is your due in the fulfillment of a complete and successful life.

Sincere Good Wishes and Love,
Your Alma Heights friends.

The Alma Heights community numbered little more than 20 families but these were not just neighbours. They were good friends. Those who took part in the writing of this letter without doubt included Grace Campbell and Wilma Dunn, who lived nearby while the way the letter is written suggests the work of Annie Campbell who was also the pianist/organist for the church services. I'm sure mom valued it, as I do also.

For this section of her life, I kept all my letters from her and to her as well as letters to and from Norman and Gordon, so I have a fuller account of these years than from any other period of her long experience.

Time for new endeavours

I say these were the best years of her life because she was free to do the things that gave her the most pleasure. She had her car so she was able to move around freely, coming down to see us in Lively as well as her local travels. She had the joy of fellowship and study and learning at the Thessalon Bible Chapel, her ministry at the Algoma Manor and still enjoyed the fellowship of her friends in Alma Heights.

Getting down family history

All her time was not spent on Christian materials. There are loads of handwritten notes about her family background, and thorough research of her family tree. There are notes from relatives to whom she had written to get the most complete information, so that for most of the relations we have accurate dates of birth and death and locality.

As she aged and began to have more trouble with sight and hearing and memory as I will record later, she wrote and rewrote her life story, so that the family could know our background. As a result, I received multiple accounts of her family and her life which has allowed me to verify the things she felt were important.

She filled scrapbooks with poems and readings, news articles and obituaries. In 1979 she wrote to me. "I spent a week getting my scrapbooks all up to date, another week on my photograph albums, and another on the history of our families."

When our sisters-in-law had to clean out her place in 1984, she had cupboards full of material. From this whole period of time, her many notebooks are full of verses of scripture which she wrote out because these verses touched her heart. She kept detailed notes on the sermons and bible studies at the Chapel.

This was a wonderful opportunity to at last devote her time to the things that really mattered to her. Earlier she did not have the time or opportunity; later she lost the ability to really take in the things she was trying to hold on to, but for these few years she had the time, the opportunity and the inclination to fill her days with activities of eternal value.

While some might not understand, this is who she was and this is what she loved.

Let me share with you a sample of some of the sayings that she copied into her notebooks. I suppose she must have taken these from her various reading materials.

"There are no losers with Christ and no winners with the devil."

"There are none so good that they can save themselves, and none so bad that God cannot save them."

"There may be Christians who do nothing, but there are no Christians with nothing to do."

"Years wrinkle the skin, but apathy wrinkles the soul."

"Believing Christ died - that's history; believing that Christ died for me - that's salvation."

"How empty is the life that is filled with nothing but things."

"Salvation can change the worst sinner into the most honoured saint."

Algoma Manor:

Her involvement at Algoma Manor began with visiting old friends who now lived there. Not all the residents were old. She even began finding people she had taught in early days, who came in due to poor health, dementia and other problems.

Then she got the idea that there was need for chapel services or Bible studies. Since there was no one else to provide them, she enlisted the help of Mrs. Acheson, Mrs. Tait and other friends from the Chapel, for a Tuesday afternoon gathering. I think that from the start, she invited the pastor from the Chapel or one of a number of men who willingly gave their time to share the Word of God with those in attendance. At first it was Philip Norbo, then later, Jack Correll whom the residents quickly came to really appreciate. Jack had a real love for these folks, going early to visit them before the chapel time.

Each service consisted of the singing of a number of hymns, prayer and message. She sometimes had a soloist as well. These meetings carried on all the time she was capable of leading them, continued when she was no longer able to do so, and continue to this day.

Her pattern, I believe, was to go the Manor just after the noon hour, visiting with various ones and inviting them to come at 2:00 p.m. Where people were in wheelchairs, she often pushed their chairs to the meeting room. Soon these meetings were attended by 30 to 50 or more residents each week.

When Sheila and I would come for a visit she would take us off to the Manor with the strong suggestion that Sheila and I sing for the folk. I was not always happy to do this because it looked to me like mom pushing her boy, a Baptist Pastor, of whom she was so proud. I remember at least one time when I refused, and in a following letter got thoroughly scolded for my unwillingness.

Mom Hern serving the Lord in her later years***

Other Christian activities

In her home she also started a weekly Bible study which carried on for years. The teaching was done by ladies she knew who were able to explain the Word for those who attended. Numbers were never large, but ladies from a wide variety of backgrounds came regularly, learning to enjoy studying the Bible together.

This was her week: Sunday morning and evening services, Tuesday gathering at the Manor, Wednesday evening Bible Study at the Chapel, Thursday evening Bible Study at the house and in between, her personal reading of the Bible, Christian books, and other good material.

Over the years she collected quite a library of Christian books which I inherited when she went into the Manor herself. I was amazed to see how marked up these books were, showing how she was trying to absorb their content. Like myself she was disappointed that she couldn't seem to retain what she had read. For a period of time, she had a Good News Bible Club at her house taught by Aunt Sadie and one of the younger women from the Chapel, but after a while she found this too much and it was taken over by one of the other ladies.

With all of this, she did not turn her back on her friends from Alma Heights. It appears that the Alma Heights United Church Women gave her opportunity to teach a Bible study at some of their monthly meetings. With them she worked through studies regarding the Creation, followed by the Gospel of John.

Her motivation

Of all she simply says "I am trying to make good use of the borrowed time I have been given and I praise the Lord for the strength He has given me, when I see so many younger than I am that are in such a sad state."

I understand her desire to be useful to her Lord and to people during these later years of life because Sheila and I feel the same way. Do you see why these were her best years?

Nearer but still far away

From the moment that Sheila and I went to Toronto, followed by our various pastorates, we were never around to minister to the needs of our parents. How thankful we have always been for our brothers and sisters-in-law, who so faithfully assisted in whatever way necessary through all these years. Meanwhile Sheila's sister and brother-in-law did the same for her parents.

Being closer during those few years in Lively, Ontario from 1971 - 1977 meant that Sheila and I could visit more often in Thessalon or on the Island with Sheila's parents. Of course, when in Thessalon, we stayed with mom but we also wanted to spend time with Gordon and Marge and Norman and Jean. She encouraged this, and we were glad for this time with them. Spending time with them cut down on time with mom so she often felt shortchanged.

When we were visiting over a weekend, Sheila and I liked to attend the morning service at our home church, First Baptist Church in the Sault. How good it was to listen to our beloved Pastor Macgregor once again. This dear man for years sent us the church bulletin every week, addressed in his own handwriting. We loved those bulletins because they contained the Pastor's own news report on the comings and goings of the church family. How he looked after a church of 300, keeping up with visitation of the church families, preparation of messages for the adult Bible Class, the morning and evening services and Wednesday Bible Study, all without help, is more than I know. After 35 years as Pastor of First Baptist, he and Mrs. Macgregor finally retired at the end of 1980. We still miss his benediction, "Grace, mer-r-rcy and peace," a hang on burr from his youth in Scotland.

As you can see, there was never adequate time to spend with her, but there was one other draw back of always living far from home. Unlike Norm's kids who were able to visit with her or see her often, our children never really got to know their grandma very well, nor did she have opportunity to really know them well.

While we know she loved them, her strong interest in spiritual things, and in the churches I served seemed to take priority.

So what do our children remember?

Juanita writes, "I think I remember Grandpa Hern just a little, or maybe it's just the picture we have of sitting on his lap. I have very vague memories of the old farmhouse but nothing concrete."

"She always had petunias in her front garden, her garage was stuffed with all kinds of stuff and her back room was stuffed with all kinds of stuff too. She made those really good peanutbutter/butterscotch squares with marshmallows."

"She had a wonderful old pump organ that I played often. And I remember that we woke up really early one time we stayed there to watch Princess Di getting married on TV.

"I remember being at Uncle Norm's at Christmas. We went snowmobiling and also went on a sleigh ride behind the horses"

Ian has fewer memories. He writes, "One of my strongest memories of her is how she was always whistling." Mom wasn't much of a whistler, so it was always a quite breathy sound, that obviously stuck with a little boy.

A Birthday Celebration

1975 was the year that she was upset with her friend Muriel McPhee for throwing an 80th birthday party for her, because now everyone knew how old she was!

Muriel was a life long friend, as different from mom as she could possibly be. Muriel was always rushing here and there. She was always laughing, and her flame red hair (straight out of a bottle), and jaunty ways were as much a part of her, as mom's spiritual involvement was of her.

In 1979, though Muriel was experiencing severe health problems and was very thin, she insisted on going to Texas for the winter as usual. Seeing her off, her friends sensed that they might not see her again, and this proved true. She died there where her body was cremated and brought back to the Thessalon area. Mom had lost a real, true and lifelong friend and felt it deeply.

The beginning of health problems

It was about this time that she also began to experience difficulties with her own health. In 1975, she began to have a recurring problem with skin cancer, and a loss of her old-time energy.

We began to hear of problems with her sight and her hearing. "My hearing is such a problem, and unless I watch their lips, I just don't know what they are saying. I got another hearing aid, so if this doesn't show an improvement, I guess I'll just give up trying and accept it all as it is. X-rays on my neck and shoulder, and blood tests, all proved o.k., so the doctor seems to think I'm a pretty healthy old girl."

Another move

In early 1977, we dropped the bombshell that we were visiting Kamloops, B.C. with a view to a call to that city, so far removed from Ontario.

In a letter she said, "As to the possibility of your moving away, this hit me hard, but I realize we can't pin you down to one place if the Lord wants you to go elsewhere." Later she wrote, "After the initial shock, I began to see God's leading in this... you have your own life to lead and I only want God's plan for you to be fulfilled. I can't praise Him enough for your decision to serve Him in the ministry, so cheer up and don't worry anymore about leaving me."

It was not only mom who was affected by this move. It was difficult for Sheila's mom and dad also to lose the close contact with our three kids, especially as these were their only grandchildren, and our kids were always closer to them than to my mother. Taking our children away from their grandparents has been the one of the few regrets about our move to B.C.

When we were about ready to go, my brothers and their families threw a party for us, at which they presented us with a watercolour picture of dad's cottage. What a great choice, bringing such fond memories to both Sheila and myself of times spent there with dad.

To travel across the country to our new location, one of the men from the church in Lively and his wife volunteered to drive the U-Haul while we came with van and tent trailer. Our children were 9, 7 and 3 ½. One of Sheila's aunts, Aunt Betty, did up bags for the children with something to be opened each day. These were greatly appreciated and helpful.

As we wended our way across the prairies, one thing was looked forward to. All the way, Ian talked about going "through the mountains." Unfortunately, when we actually came to the mountains, he was so sick that he missed seeing the tunnels, which in a small degree, took us "through the mountains."

Contact from afar

Not too long after we left, a rash of visitors came from the west. Cousin Reba Hern came from Vancouver and Mom's oldest brother, his daughter and son-in-law and their daughter came from Innisfail, Alberta. This was such an enjoyable visit but, with our leaving, their visiting plus Norm and Jean's anniversary, mom wrote that, "I just feel like sleeping all the time. I just can't take the confusion."

Very quickly we saw the challenges of moving so far from family, because about the time we arrived, Sheila's dad had health problems and we were unable to be there.

Changes for the whole family

As it turned out, 1977 proved to be a year of major change for Norman and Jean, and for Gordon and Marge, as well as ourselves.

Norm sold the Rogers farm to his son Keith, and they moved into Bruce Mines. Norm got work with the Department of Highways which continued until his retirement. Meanwhile, Gordon and Marge sold their cows and milk quota in favour of a quieter life with fewer chores.

We, on our part, settled into a new church called Dallas Barnhartvale Baptist on the east end of Kamloops, B.C. and had a house built into which we moved at the end of December.

In March of 1978, mom came to Kamloops for a visit. Her oldest brother Leonard had been seriously ill. She hoped to stop and see him, but unfortunately, he passed away and was buried before she could get there. That was a great sorrow. It was lovely to have her and it gave more time for the kids and her to spend time together.

In each of our pastorates, her visits allowed her to not only see our work but enter into a real friendship with some of the people. So it was once again in Kamloops. People like the Homer Bloomfields, the Scales and others became personal friends, allowing her to form an emotional attachment to the church.

On her way home, she was able to visit with our cousins in Alberta which was really nice so she had a very good trip.

In May, Gordon and Marge also arrived for a good visit which we enjoyed so very much. Gordon helped with terracing our lot and in other ways in equipping our new home.

Then an unexpected occurrence: Sheila and I decided to make the trip across the country by bus with the three children. Sheila's parents were really feeling the loss of the grandchildren. The bus took 3 ½ days each way, out of three weeks, but it was worth it. Ian and I came back early so I could lead a Seniors Camp while Sheila, Juanita and Darryl stayed on a little longer.

Watching the family grow

Holding mom's attention during this whole period were weddings. Isabel and Ron, Phyllis Ann and John. Still to come were Keith and Rosemary, Beth and Kevin, Glen and Laurie and Jenat and Clint. In Marge and Gordon's family, Donald and Benda and Bruce and Nora also married during these years. Of course, it was not long before great grandchildren began appearing on the scene, bringing a new level of interest into her life.

In August 1978, two of her brother Clarence's children, Clyde and Lorilyn and Linda and Sid were married in a double wedding ceremony in the Sault.

As these years slipped by, however, it was evident that mom was aging, with more and more trips to see the eye doctor and the hearing specialist. She began reporting dizzy spells. We wonder if these were the precursors of the small strokes that affected sight and hearing still more. In her driver's test in 1978 when she was 83 years, she reported that both eyes and ears were a problem. Still she got her licence and kept up her active lifestyle.

It wasn't just mom who was experiencing more problems. Letters told of neighbours and long time friends experiencing major health problems or dying. Letters were filled with news of Aunt Sadie's many falls, an operation for a malignant tumour and other times in hospital.

Sheila's dad was also operated on, resulting in a colostomy bag with all its attendant difficulties. Still, Tom Simpson retained his quiet uncomplaining demeanor, an example to us all of how to respond to less desirable experiences.

Mom was with us again through Christmas 1980 when she stayed for 2 ½ months waiting for the new church to be opened. In the end she had to go home before the February '81 dedication, but she was so glad to be home. What a warm welcome she received from her friends at the Chapel and the Manor. "So lovely to know you are wanted and needed. I'm galloping around here again like I always did."

In the summer of 1981, we made another trip home to Ontario, enjoying the visit.

And so, these 10 years passed by. Good years, filled with purpose. These would continue for a while longer but the day came when she herself had to go into the manor as a resident. As you will hear, this brought on terrible stress and more physical problems, but once again that is material for my next - and final chapter of a life not lived in vain.

Chapter Fourteen

Heading Home

Heaven is not a figment of imagination.
It is not a feeling or an emotion.
It is not the "Beautiful Isle of Somewhere."
It is a prepared place for a prepared people.
Dr. David Jeremiah

For the Christian, heaven is where Jesus is.
We do not need to speculate on what heaven will be like.
It is enough to know that we will be forever with Him.
William Barclay

As I work with Seniors, it seems to me that one needs a sense of humour to age well.

Such a sense of humour was demonstrated by Julie Andrews of "Sound of Music" fame, as she redid the words of "My Favourite Things." Invited to make a special appearance at Manhattan's Radio City Music Hall, Julie introduced and sang a new set of lyrics for that well-known song. Listen in with me.

Maalox and nose drops and needles for knitting,
Walkers and handrails and new dental fittings,
Bundles of magazines tied up in string,
These are a few of my favorite things.
Cadillacs and cataracts and hearing aids and glasses,
Polident and Fixodent and false teeth in glasses,
Pacemakers, golf carts and porches with swings,
These are a few of my favorite things.
When the pipes leak, When the bones
creak, When the knees go bad,
I simply remember my favorite things,
and then I don't feel so bad.

Hot tea and crumpets and corn pads for bunions,
No spicy hot food or food cooked with onions,
Bathrobes and heating pads and hot meals they bring,
These are a few of my favorite things.
Back pains, confused brains, and no need for sinnin',
Thin bones and fractures and hair that is thinnin',
And we won't mention our short shrunken frames,
When we remember our favorite things.

When the joints ache, When the hips
break, When the eyes grow dim,
Then I remember the great life I've had,
and then I don't feel so bad.

Julie Andrews was celebrating her 69th birthday when she sang this humorous ditty. In 1982 mom was celebrating her 87th. That's a significant difference, so while people in their 80's and 90's may have a chuckle at Julie's humour, there are times when these later years don't seem so funny.

Mom was still in relatively good shape as she entered this period but as I wrote in Chapter Thirteen her best years were behind her.

Still an independent lady

Mom had been determined all her life to never get old, and as I quoted in the last chapter, she reported that she was "galloping around here again like I always did."

Still, there were problems developing that threatened that sense of well being.

Radiation treatments in Toronto on a spot of skin cancer, the start of a series of small strokes, increasing difficulties with vision and hearing, hospitalization with jaundice and later with shingles. Spread over these last eight years, all of these were taking enjoyment out of daily living.

Repeated trips to the eye doctor and hearing specialists in the Sault brought no relief. In a letter early in 1984, "I really like to read and write still but my eyes and ears really give me problems. Boy, what a time - I'm a blurry creature and I don't just enjoy trying to do things any more. I don't drive my car and I can't walk very far without getting so tired. But I hope I'll soon get my nerves settled."

As I mentioned earlier in relation to dad, my own age is revealing more of what they went through in later years. I am not sure that Optometry at that time was yet diagnosing macular degeneration, which twists the letters on the printed page. In mom's trips to the optometrist, there was no mention of macular degeneration, but I wonder now if that is what was giving her 'blurry eyes'. I have it and I have to be especially careful when reading the numbers in the phone book. Diminished hearing and hearing aids that don't seem to help me either, leading my wife to jibe me about 'selective hearing'. I can appreciate more and more the problems mom faced.

In December of '82, she "took a spell with cold, clammy sweats and really frightened myself." The doctor's advice to Gordon was, "Keep an eye on her for the next few days. She is so independent, she might not tell you."

Ah, yes, so independent. That was mother. Strong minded would be another expression which could be used. Her response was, "Well I don't want to be a bother to my family. I'm really w+ell looked after, only once in a while I get to know I'm not as young as I used to be, and my old body is beginning to wear out. But I've been on borrowed time for 17 years now. The Lord has been so gracious to me regarding my health, but it might not always be so."

Sustained by faith

This was her other side. Her strong faith in the Lord, and desire to serve Him kept her going.

She rejoiced in a number of new ladies who were coming to the Bible Study at her house or to the Coffee Hour at the Chapel. I was familiar with all of these ladies and pleasantly surprised to hear of their growing interest. Most of these had been faithful church attenders, but realized that they really didn't know the Word of God very well, and now found learning quite fascinating.

She continued to give leadership to the Tuesday afternoon Bible Study at the Manor and to attend Sunday morning and evening services at the Chapel.

She also continued to take a deep interest in everything that was happening in our lives here in Kamloops, especially in the church. Progress in the church and at Sunnybrae Bible

Camp excited her. "I just delight to hear how things are going so well at your church. I am so thankful I just can't keep from weeping at times."

But her faith caused her to worry a lot, too. She prayed constantly for her family's salvation and worried over what seemed to her to be a lack of spiritual interest. She loved every one of her children and grandchildren and believed passionately in the return of the Lord and the dangers of not being ready to meet Him. While she didn't have the courage to witness to them, I doubt that there were any of the family who did not feel the pressure of her concern.

Was her concern helpful? Probably not. In 1972 while preparing a message for my congregation in Lively, I felt the desire to write a letter of witness to brother Norman. Shortly, I received a 12-page letter from him.

"Dear Allen, for sometime (a long time, to be exact) I have felt that we were sort of feeling each other out. ... it seemed that sooner or later we would go to bat against each other, so I guess the time has arrived. I am going to say right on the start that I have respected your choice of life's goal, even though I can't agree with many of your views."

He illustrated his difference of opinion by references to relatives whose Baptist faith he did not envy. "I don't want you to think that I am trying to defend the United Church, but I feel that if we all lived up to the teachings of it, we would all be a lot better off than we are." At the same time, he acknowledged that he was gradually losing interest in church. "I wouldn't think of denouncing religion or anything like that but interest has waned just a bit...By now you are probably so disgusted with me that you would disown me if you could."

In fact, when I read his letter, I cried, because this was my brother whom I had always looked up to. Many of his criticisms of myself, and our evangelical faith, were on point. I could identify with them as having substance.

I could understand fully his feeling because I remember well the days before I became involved at the Chapel. I remember my own reactions to some of those Brethren people and their faith. Even after mom and I began attending, and began hearing words like "being saved" or "born again" or "converted" and other evangelical language, I found that language strange. These were not words with which I was familiar, and I felt uncomfortable. But as I listened to the Word of God, and as I began to read the Bible for myself, I began to recognize that these words were used in the Bible and were alright. Now, I am aware that as a pastor, this manner of speaking is part of my make up, and probably makes friends and family as uncomfortable as I used to be.

But at the same time, Norm was also mistaken in his reactions. You see, it is impossible to really know God or understand His ways if we do not read or hear His Word. Without that, we have only our own ideas which are untrustworthy about who God is or what He is like. We could not know Him apart from what He has revealed about Himself. He revealed Himself to "holy men as they were moved by the Holy Spirit" and they wrote down what they learned in the book we call the Bible.

The second way in which He has revealed Himself is through His Son, Jesus, who came from heaven to earth and lived a sinless life among us. His story, too, is written down in the Bible.

That is why we need to attend a church where the Bible is believed and preached. As we begin to understand the Word, and finally to yield our lives to the Lord Jesus, it does change the way we think and act.

We are often misunderstood as thinking that we are better than others, but such is not the case. Far from feeling superior, true Christians come to that point of acknowledging failures and shortcomings, and sinfulness. We confess that we deserved God's judgment, and that if Jesus had not paid for our failures by giving His life for us, we would be cut off from God forever.

Far from believing that we are 'good' or 'better than others', we know that there is no goodness in us, and, therefore, we need to turn to God for forgiveness and salvation.

We have failed in the past, still fall short in the present, and apart from God's grace and mercy would fail in the future. Romans 5:8 *"But God demonstrates His own love toward us, in that while we were still sinners, Christ died for us."*

This was mom's concern and mine. We desire that every one of our loved ones may know the joy of being forgiven and being on the way to heaven. I fear that the real stumbling block is that human beings do not want to believe that they are sinners who need a Saviour. That message has been offensive to people ever since Jesus confronted the religious people two thousand years ago, and remains the same today.

A busy year - 1983

1983 found her still on the go, enjoying a visit from Reba Hern from Vancouver.

Granddaughters Beth and Jenat were each married. Then in early summer, Mom, Gordon and Marge, and Norman and Jean and nephew Ken all came west to visit with us. What a great time!

As mom said after they got home, "It was good to see you all again. The children are growing up and soon will be off on their own."

In December she wrote to tell us, "Suddenly I went dizzy and I felt a bit nauseated. I got into the bathroom and had to hang on to the basin as I was afraid of falling. I sat quietly and the sensation passed off in about 10 minutes, so I got into bed. I felt it might have been a heart attack, but it passed off in bed."

Gordon and Marge wrote of changes. "She has been getting these headaches and her heart has been fibrillating and sending minute blood clots to the brain, and she is now showing small signs of confusion, mixing up her pronouns, though she laughs them off. "

1984 -A very difficult year

1984 started off with more concerns about her overall health. During those months leading up to the summer, we were conscious of her growing confusion as we talked to her on the phone. We knew that it was not an easy time for our brothers and their wives as she was needing to be taken for appointments which were not helping, and as Marge said in a letter, "She has let her nerves get the better of her."

It was a time to encourage her and as you now know, that which blessed her most was the Word of God. I reminded her that as Christians, we have a glorious inheritance, and while trials come, they have a purpose. First Peter 1:7 reminds us, *"that the trial of your faith, being much more precious than gold that perishes, though it be tried with fire, might be found unto praise and honour and glory at the appearing of Jesus Christ..."*

I wrote, "Praise the Lord, we don't suffer without purpose - and the purpose is that our faith may grow and we may bring glory to the Lord. We are weak, we fail, but God's grace is sufficient and He is keeping us day by day."

I shared with her about the children's progress: "Juanita is writing her Grade 8 piano exam this summer and will be qualified to teach piano when she feels able to do so. The boys are both taking lessons this year and I believe are enjoying it."

In April I wrote, "Today is Juanita's 16th birthday. She takes everything in her stride so well. She will be getting her learner's driving permit, so we should have an interesting time in the next few months."

I know that mom believed that the grace of God was sufficient, but the summer was going to test that belief supremely, and I would be the very cause of that test. Looking back, I wonder if we could have done things in a much better way than we did, but as we were going home for a visit, the family had decided that she needed to enter the Algoma Manor as a resident, and since I was "the fair haired boy", I was the one to help her make that transition.

Unfortunately, we had limited time and so I pushed her toward that decision - for which she was not ready. Stress and confusion brought her to the verge of collapse.

A year later she wrote, "You all thought you were doing right but, in the end, I was heartbroken and from mid-August, I lived in a world by myself. By the time I came into the Manor, I was sick in body and soul."

I am sharing all of this because many families face these difficulties at some point, and in dealing with seniors I try to encourage them to make the changes while it is still under their own control. Waiting till the family have to make those decisions will often bring on this kind of distress because others don't feel the same about your possessions as you do yourself. The following three months were difficult as she tried to designate her various things to different ones. Knowing that she could not organize her things as she would like but have to let the girls do it was a great distress to her. Gathering her things together and trying to decide what to keep was a great challenge to Jean and Marge as well, and not one which mom handled well.

I remember my brother Norm trying to console her, "Today it's you, mom, but tomorrow it will be me." No words, however, were sufficient to overcome the shock of being uprooted, and I believe mom came close to a nervous breakdown during this time of adjustment.

On November 1, she moved in, finding the trauma of moving from a three-bedroom house full of all her things to one room shared with another woman. "My things are crowded in a space 9 feet by 14 feet with a small table, a chest of 3 drawers and my chair."

Later in the month I wrote to her, "When we got home this summer, and saw how upset and confused you were, we understood why Norman and Gordon had decided that we really needed to start the ball rolling to secure a place for you. I hope you will be able to come to the point of forgiving us in that matter. At least now we know that you will be getting proper meals and care, and that is worth something."

In response she wrote, "I had to just bunch my stuff together. Anna (Stewart) helped me so much not only to plan but to move me. Jack (Correll), and Allen and Lucy McDougall (friends from the Bible Chapel) all shared with me but what a mess - nothing was in order. I can't find the things I most need."

"One night when I was trying to sleep, the door opened and Dr. Parfait and the nurse came in. I jumped up when I saw him and burst into tears and for an hour or more, I cried my heart out to him in my trouble. I was completely exhausted from work and worry. My condition must have worsened. For days everyone knew I was at the end of the line and I really do believe I had another stroke. My hearing and seeing got worse and my memory is terrible.

"However, I found myself whistling this morning. I surprised myself. I almost laughed out."

By December, there was evidence of improvement. "I have made a good recovery though I tire out easily. I just had to sleep until I was rested. I haven't tried wheeling people around as I tire easily. However, I have been around Normal Care and Bed Care, talking to each of them. After my prolonged absence they seem glad to have me back around." She reports that "grand daughter Phyllis has a new boy, and Beth is expecting in February", which shows that she was taking an interest in things, and she expressed her desire to look after her own business affairs once again.

And so, 1984, a difficult year, closed with hope for a brighter tomorrow.

Life in the Manor

How thankful we are for good homes for our Seniors such as the Algoma Manor. At the same time, we should not be so naive as to believe that it is easy for people who have been independent all their lives to enter into an institutional setting.

As mom settled in, there was evidence of overall improvement. "Anna (Stewart), the head nurse and a dear

Christian friend always says, 'Mabel, you have to be a witness here,' so with her help, I can be helpful."

"As to my hearing I am no better, so I don't go to the sitting room, not being able to hear. I enjoy my own rocking chair. They gave me a board I can put across the arms so I can sit and write or do what I choose. I have also been able to visit with some of the women, and share with them a little about the Lord."

In June of '85, I was able to be home for Mom's 90th birthday party, held at the Manor. A good number of relatives and friends rejoiced with her in this milestone.

"I look hale and hearty and everyone tells me how well I look, but when you can't hear and see, it's a poor life. When the family comes in and everyone gets talking, I just can't stand the noise and have to go to my room."

After her birthday, she received a wonderful letter from her niece Enid Sharpe in Innisfail. The letter started off, "There is a bond between us that space or time cannot transcend."

Isabel Moore, her niece from Red Deer also wrote. Both letters brought her up to date on the families, and must have been a great encouragement as she always felt close to her brother's family.

She wrote, "I am thankful for the way the Lord has cared for me and pray that He will lead me to the end."

"I know not what the future hath of marvel or surprise. Assured alone that life and death his mercy underlies."

In December of 1985, we took the family home to Manitoulin Island where Sheila's dad was suffering from cancer. As a family we were happy that the kids could spend time with their grandparents, enjoying Christmas traditions.

While we were there, we experienced a heavy winter storm with wind and lots snow. We were especially thankful to be there as Sheila's dad passed away in April of 1986.

February 8, 1986 was Aunt Sadie's birthday, and mom was able to write and give a tribute to her at her birthday party in the Manor.

In the fall of '86, we were on the move again, after accepting a call to Eagle Mountain Baptist Church in Port Moody, a small church of about 40 people where we established an outreach centre which we called Harmony House, "bringing harmony to homes, families and community." Mom found this a bit confusing as she could no longer visualize our new circumstances.

In July of '87, mom had a wonderful surprise. Linda Coventry Lewis from Coquitlam came to see her. "I just dropped my washing and we just hugged each other until I got it into my head that this was real and not a vision or something.... She was a dear pupil and I shall always cherish my remembrance of her." Then she had the blessing of a visit from her niece and nephew, Jim and Enid Sharpe from Alberta as well.

January '88 brought Sheila and I home once more, this time for her mother's funeral. With Tom gone and now her mom gone as well, it was a sad time for her. Again, how glad we were that her sister Jane was nearby to care for them but we regretted the fact that Sheila had not been able to be there with each of her parents before they were taken.

Her Closing Years

In the fall of '88, we were able to tell mom of Ian being in Bible School and of Juanita's engagement to be married.

In January of '89, I flew home for a week, but found it hard to see mom so confused, even unable to dress herself properly. I wrote letters to all the grandchildren following my visit. "It is sad that people get old and can't do the things they used to do but I want you to know that they weren't always old. One time they were boys and girls just like you and loved to play like you do. Can you imagine Grandma Hern being a young girl and playing ball or skipping, or combing her doll's hair?"

We rejoiced that Norman and Jean and Gordon and Marge brought mom out to Coquitlam for the August wedding. It was a lovely wedding and we were glad she could be present, but as she wrote when she got home, "I didn't make the best of it. I couldn't hear. I missed so much. The wedding was something to be remembered. Juanita and Terry were all very nice. Ian and Darryl have grown up."

Although she seemed to perk up a bit after the trip, she did not do well in her remaining year.

In March, '90 she visited Anna Stewart, and wanted her to write for her but couldn't remember what she desired to write and just sat in the rocking chair rocking. "She doesn't talk much anymore and is so restless."

Granddaughter Phyllis worked at the Manor and writes, "Seeing lots of Grandma was nice but it also had its draw backs. Seeing her deteriorate slowly was not the easiest time of my life. Near the last part of her life she quite often didn't know who I was which I found extremely hard to take."

In November, Marge reported that she had to be tied into the chair and with the sides up on the bed. "She still knows everyone but she is just tired out."

Heading Home

We have all experienced the joy of heading for our own home after being away for a while. But the idea of heading home takes on another meaning for Christians in the later stages of life or when facing severe illness, as they tell you that they are longing "to go home," which represents the end of a long struggle, and the beginning of that new, fuller, more glorious life with the one who has "gone before to prepare us a place for us."

In December, 1990, Mom slipped away into the presence of her Lord and Saviour.

Her funeral was held at the Thessalon Bible Chapel with Jack Correll preaching the message. I had the privilege of singing a solo and giving the memories of my mother.

She was buried in the Pine Grove Cemetery at Little Rapids, Ontario alongside her husband.

We've come a long piece since "a small, auburn haired girl stood well back from the banks of the Little Thessalon River, with her heart in her mouth, watching the cows swim across the river from the neighbour's farm."

We have travelled 95 years since that little girl was born and yet we really haven't travelled far at all, because we have come back to that same Little Thessalon River, just a little further away, to a cemetery not far from its banks.

As we have shared Mom and Dad's story, we have seen two lives which travelled through almost one hundred years of great changes. Like so many others of their contemporaries, they had experienced two world wars, a great depression and a life of hard work. They moved through an era when horses or the train were the chief means of travel, homes were lit by lamplight, and cows were milked by hand. They entered the era of electricity, of milking machines, of tractor powered farm machinery and newer and newer automobiles. One room schools with eight grades were the norm in rural areas. Life was hard, and money was never more than just enough. Through it all, they lived lives of honesty and integrity setting an example for their offspring.

I am so glad that dad had those quiet years at the lake as a fulfillment of his life.

I am glad that mom had those last years of reward in the opportunity to show care and concern for many older lives. We have seen a woman who had a great love and concern for every one of her children, grandchildren and great grandchildren. She was a woman who loved the Lord Jesus Christ with all her heart. Her greatest desire was to see her entire family able to enjoy a personal relationship with Jesus with the assurance of heaven. That was her constant prayer and her greatest worry.

Theirs were not perfect lives, but I thank God for them. I also thank God also for Sheila's parents. Each of these two couples left **a good heritage.**

You were their heritage: as **Psalm 127:3 says, "Behold, children are a heritage from the LORD. The fruit of the womb is a reward."**

Their lives left a heritage of honesty and integrity worthy of following.

But we have a still greater heritage: The Bible says in Psalm 119:111 *"Your testimonies (your Word) I have taken as a heritage forever, for they are the rejoicing of my heart.'*

About the author

 llen Hern grew up on a dairy farm in northern Ontario, near the small town of Thessalon, and fifty miles east of Sault Ste. Marie.

A near death experience from a ruptured appendix brought the 19-year-old to the awareness of his mortality. "Nineteen-year olds don't die. Old people die. Right?"

It also brought him to an awareness of spiritual need. "If I ever were near death, I would have time for an eleventh-hour conversion, wouldn't I?

This led to a five-and-a-half-year teaching career which included a radical change of thinking and a new direction for life. It also included marriage to Sheila, his delightful and faithful wife of 56 years.

Pastoral ministry included two churches in Ontario, (Port Perry and Lively) and four in British Columbia, (Kamloops, Port Moody, Kelowna and Lake Cowichan) From there he and his wife semi-retired to Kamloops in 2008, where he served another ten years as associate pastor of First Baptist Church. In 2018, he retired again after 50 years in ministry.

Allen and Sheila have three children, nine grandchildren and one great grandchild. "Some of our greatest blessings call us Nana and Papa." A note of great sadness, and yet of great joy is the reality that God has called two of their grandchildren, Emily and Joshua into the fullness of His glory and the everlasting joy of His presence. Yet He has also given them the most delightful grand-daughter-in-law.

In retirement he and Sheila continue to live in Kamloops where he has written two biographies.

The first is this tribute to his parents.

The second as yet unpublished memoir is entitled "**Challenge and Change – the Travails and Joys of a Complex Woman**". Follow his much older cousin through ordination as the second woman ordained into the ministry of the United Church of Canada in 1937. Her 13-year ministry ended in burnout and five years in a Catholic Convent. During her subsequent 16 years as a teacher of Religious Knowledge and English in the Government High School in Nassau, the Bahamas, she began travelling the world which continued into her retirement in Tsawwassen, B.C. It is a fascinating story. Ask for notification of its publication.

You may reach Allen and Sheila at # 13, 1285 14th Street, Kamloops, B.C., V2C 8K9

hern@telus.net   1-250-376-1607

For those who are interested, the author has written a small appendix to this book called **"Handsful of Honey"**, which he would gladly send to any requesting it.